The Edwardians and Beyond 1901 – 1939:

Social History for Family Historians

By Kate Juffs

KATE JUFFS.

THE EDWARDIANS AND BEYOND, 1901 – 1939:

SOCIAL HISTORY FOR FAMILY HISTORIANS

TABLE OF CONTENTS:

TABLE OF PHOTOGRAPHS:

Dedication

For Edith Bessie Lardner (1895 – 1976) and Ada Lylie Thompson (1910 – 1998) who lived through these fascinating times.

1. Introduction

For the first part of the twentieth century a person who didn't break the laws of England and Wales could go through life with almost no contact with the state beyond the post office and the policeman. There was no requirement to have a passport when one travelled to and from the continent, no form of driving test or licence was required to drive a car, or even for the car itself. There were no official numbers, no identity cards or indeed any form of identity required at all.

A wealthy person might be called to serve upon a jury, to vote, or to pay taxes but for the poor even these were not required. A man could choose whether to fight to defend his country, or to remain living in the country where no politicians or anyone living outside his locality even knew he existed. Years could pass without any state intervention in people's lives.

The state did intervene from time to time: there was a requirement for children to go to school and laws to curb excessive working hours for women and children plus a few others, but they were very few and far between.

The outbreak of World War I in 1914 changed all this. From then onward the state started to dictate how people should live and how they should work and play. Things had changed forever.

This book concentrates on how the majority of people lived, those in the working- and middle-classes. Their lives changed almost beyond recognition throughout this period of time. The aim of this book is to fill in the gaps between the birth, marriage, death certificates and census returns. It considers the houses, food, entertainment, work and unemployment of the time. For many there was the hardship of poverty and this was the time that saw the end of the horrendous poor laws.

Throughout the book there are references to pounds (£), shillings (s) and pence (d), which was the currency used during this period. A list of the various coins are given in section 14.1.1, but for now suffice it to say that there were 12 pence in one shilling and twenty shillings in one pound. At the point of decimalisation in 1972 one shilling was equivalent to five new pence.

I hope that you will find you can either read through this book from start to finish or you can dip in and read the subjects that interest you. The extensive table of contents is at the start of the book to help you find the section you require.

Happy reading to you all.

2.   The Home

In the early twentieth century, before the onset of the First World War, the large Victorian houses that lined countless streets of urban and rural Britain were seen as fussy and overly ornate. Their dark interiors were oppressive and dull, and for many who now had to live without the help of paid servants they were difficult to clean and maintain. The whims of the Victorians were out of fashion; something elegant and simple was desired. Working men and women were keen to establish their own homes and for the first time there was a little money left over from the hard slog of simply surviving.

People wanted comfort. Large drafty, rambling houses were expensive to keep and people wanted homes with modern amenities; running water, electricity and central heating. Large Victorian houses were expensive to adapt. The answer was to build cheap, modern small houses to replace the poor housing of the inter cities. But the population was growing fast, from 15 million at the start of the Victorian age in 1837 to 32.5 million in 1901 and 40.0 million by 1931, and builders couldn't keep up with demand.

But it was not only the houses themselves that were changing. People wanted more furniture and that furniture had to be comfortable. They were spending more time in their homes than ever before and, for the first time, they had choices. Laboursaving devices were being marketed, giving women freedom from daily chores and increasing leisure time.

The changes that happened did so, like all fashions, slowly as the years progressed. As the fashions changed so too did the houses they left behind, giving us a glimpse into the world of our ancestors.

2.1.   In the Home

2.1.1.   Pre-war

In the first decade of the twentieth century homes were sombre, dark places where people rested and lived, little changed from the late Victorian era.

Upper working class homes followed a pattern, very similar, showing very little of their tenants' lives. A wooden front door with stained glass windows greeted householders and visitors alike. There would have been patterned, dark wallpaper and tiled floors, with an umbrella stand and perhaps a coat rack that stood on the floor, draped with heavy coats. The smell of bees wax and potpourri would have hung in the air, together with cooking smells coming from the kitchen at the back of the house.

A door off the hallway would lead to the neat and tidy parlour, kept for visitors and friends that the owners wanted to impress. It was the first, and possibly the only, room that a visitor would see. As a result it was barely used, but it was an indication that the family was reasonably well off and as such everyone aspired to have one, whether it was used or not. The furniture was heavy and dark, the stale smell of cigars and cigarette smoke hanging in the air, so ingrained that even the potpourri wouldn't mask the smell.

Next was the family room, where the family congregated. This was likely to be the largest room in the house with a table in the middle, surrounded by wooden chairs and perhaps a more comfortable chair for Dad. The roaring fire would light the room with a wooden rack of drying clothes and a gaggle of young children all vying for attention and food.

Next was the kitchen, small and bright with a back door leading out into the yard behind the house. Likely to be a long galley room, with cupboards and if the family was lucky a cold water tap over a large, deep ceramic sink, possibly cracked and stained in spite of many attempts to keep it clean and neat.

Cooking was done over a solid fuel stove if the family was comfortably off, or an open fire if not. Iron griddles and pans would hang from the ceiling and drying clothes and sheets would hang in the air, the smell of soap and damp clinging to everything. This was the warmest room in the house in winter and many families would to sit here to keep warm. Otherwise, if possible, the family would light a fire in the family room and would gather there, sitting at the table sharing stories of their day.

Usually the children were sent out after breakfast, either to school or to play, whatever the weather so by the evening they would be keen to eat and then hurriedly got ready for bed.

Upstairs there would be two or three bright airy bedrooms, with metal bedsteads each piled with blankets in winter. The room would be freezing in winter and boiling hot in summer. The windows would have glass, although possibly cracked in poorer homes, but there were few casements to open to let in the air. Each room was furnished sparingly. A bed, chair and possibly a chest of drawers, but little else. The room would sleep four or even five children, top to tail sleeping in one bed, and noisy arguments would be sure to break out.

On cold mornings the windows would be patterned with ice on the inside, as fires would not be lit upstairs except if a family member was ill or if the family was very wealthy. Fires were dirty and expensive and seen as unnecessary for a normal family. The inhabitants of the house would dress quickly, or even have slept in most of their day clothes for warmth, and rush downstairs to the warm kitchen or family room.

Under the bed would be a 'po or two'; A chamber pot for the use of the children and adults during the night. It was always emptied at daybreak in case the smell permeated the whole house. For the more wealthy households there might be an inside toilet and bathroom, but this was still far from common during the pre-war years. For them the toilet was outside, either a water closet near the house or an earth closet at the bottom of the yard. Washing was done in a basin in the family room each morning. Bath time was once a week, usually Saturday evening. Water heated in pots, pans and kettles was tipped into a tin bath kept for the purpose. All family members would bath in the same water, quickly jumping in after the previous occupant, hoping that the water would still be warm enough to be comfortable.

At this time many homes had gas lighting, although electric lighting and power were becoming increasingly popular. Often it was only the main rooms that had this convenience. By 1910 only two percent of homes were wired for electricity and even in those bedrooms were still lit by candle, which the occupants would take up with them when they retired for the night.

2.1.2. Homes for the poor

In Liverpool surveys of housing conditions noted that many large houses had been bought by landlords and were being let out to the poor, one family to each room. These houses were in appalling conditions. The plaster was coming off the walls, or was being held on by tatty, filthy wallpaper which bulged out under its weight. The rooms were rotting and damp, infested with vermin and in many cases there were no windows, broken floorboards and almost no furniture. Landlords refused to carry out repairs to the buildings. Rented council accommodation was almost non-existent before 1914 and so it was down to private landlords to meet the demand. Often it was widowed middle class women who had a little cash that bought houses to let out, but they didn't have the money to carry out the repairs. Or it might be that the landlords only wanted the income, not the responsibilities, so any necessary remedial work wasn't done.

Each family lived in one room, their only cooking facilities being the small fire grate in the room itself. Few pots and pans would fit into the tiny space, but they could possibly heat a little water. There were no bathrooms or inside toilets and the only facilities were the shared earth closets in the back yard. These would be stinking, filthy places, inadequate for the numbers using them. Disease spread through the families quickly once established.

The only water supply was a tap in the back yard, again sadly inadequate for the numbers who needed to use it. It would freeze up during the winter, leaving the families with no clean water supply at all. Even when the tap worked all water would have to be carried up to the room to use, often up three or four flights of uneven, rotting stairs.

It was estimated that over half a million homes in major cities in 1932 were described as unfit for human habitation. Yet, millions of people lived in conditions such as these.

Six of the most overcrowded boroughs in England and Wales were in North East England. County Durham had 20% of families, a quarter of a million people, in overcrowded homes. Liverpool had 89,000 people living two or more people to a room, and 20,000 people living three or more to a room. In St Annes 42% of families lived four or more families to a house. All in squalid, filthy conditions.

2.1.3.   After the war

When the men returned from war in 1918 or 1919 they would notice that little had changed, except perhaps that the furniture was more worn and faded, their women and children thinner and the house a little more run down. Money was tight and although their wife or mother would have kept the house clean and tidy, there would have been no shops selling furniture to replace broken items and no money for anything new. Everything had been put into the war effort. New furniture had to wait.

At the end of the First World War the government promised its returning soldiers that they would build them 'homes fit for heroes'. But the years immediately after the war were difficult and it took the government several years to get builders and local authorities to build the houses that were needed.

During the 1920s there were several efforts by parliament to encourage the building of more homes. But new projects were slow to get going and so the massive overcrowding and desperate housing shortage continued. Immediately after the war in 1919, parliament pushed through the Housing and Town Planning Act, which gave subsidies to local authorities, requiring them to survey the housing needs of people in their region and draw up plans to end overcrowding and slum dwelling. However, local authorities were slow to act on this directive and little was done.

In 1923 there was another Housing Act, this time giving local authorities and private builders a subsidy of £6 per annum for 20 years for each house built under this scheme. This proved popular and almost 500,000 houses were built over the next decade. The subsidy was increased in 1924 to £9 per annum,

In 1930 the Housing Act made provisions for slum clearance and provided subsidies from central government for rehousing families and for demolition costs. This proved to be a turning point for many people, although the improvements made were not as wonderful for the poor as they might have been.

New homes cost money and the poor could not afford a market rent for the houses being built. Private landlords, unless philanthropists, were not keen to invest money in building houses unless they would receive a good return for their money. The same applied to local authorities. The only way that rents could be reduced to affordable levels was to build homes that were smaller and cheaper than those already available.

After 1930 councils were obliged to rehouse slum dwellers and they had to set rents at lower levels so that the poor could afford them. Their answer was to build large, tall five storey blocks of small flats. Liverpool council offered such flats for 10s 6d per week, but they were unpopular with residents. The pleasant camaraderie that had been present in the slums was missing from those large blocks, even though the new homes had electricity, running water, inside toilets and baths and a lack of vermin.

By 1939 rented council accommodation comprised of 11% of all housing stock and four out of five slum dwellers had been rehoused.

2.1.4. Buying a home

As the years of the twentieth century wore on those that held onto their jobs were better off than they had even been. Many finally saw an end to their years in harsh and hateful poverty. For many home ownership was something that would put their poverty stricken days firmly behind them and ensure that they would never return. Before 1910 owner-occupiers comprised barely 10% of all British homes. By 1938 this had risen to 35%.

In the early 1920s home-ownership was very much an upper working class aspiration. At first the middle class was reluctant; it was much easier and cheaper for them to rent homes. They could move up market or to a new area much more quickly and cheaply than if they owned their home. For the working classes it was a dream.

Many buildings societies merged and expanded at this time. Halifax Permanent and Halifax Equitable merged in 1928, the Bradford and Bingley and others grew and developed. The number of families paying a mortgage rose from 554,000 in 1928 to 1.4 million in 1937. In 1910 building societies advanced £9 million in mortgages and by 1925 this had risen to £49 million. The peak was in 1936 when it reached £140 million.

Post war houses were built to a very high standard. Housewives had said, when questioned, that they wanted extra bedrooms, indoor toilets, a hot water supply, a parlour and a garden (not just a yard). They also wanted one or two separate living rooms, a separate kitchen and more space. Many people believed that they were getting ideas above their station, but the builders and local authorities listened to them.

The improved transport links to and from the centre of towns and cities meant that builders could take advantage of cheap land on the edge of cities and build there. The suburbs were advertised as having the advantages of living in the country for a low price. The move towards developing the suburbs that had started before the war continued at a rapid pace.

As the 1920s progressed the middle class also started to buy, keen to take advantage of the glamorous homes in the suburbs. Ilford, Walthamstow and Wood Green all grew from around the 1920s. Prices were advertised at £250 - £350 for a leasehold house and £350 - £450 for freehold. These large houses, of almost 1,000 square feet, could be bought by clerks and skilled workers on just £4 per week. The tramways and railways had made it possible to journey quite some distances into work, and people were keen to take advantage of reliable, cheap transport.

Cities expanded; Bristol, Birmingham, Manchester and Liverpool all had expanding suburbs in the 1920s and 30s. In the 1920s land could be bought for £100 or less per acre. This resulted in 'ribbon developments' along the main routes into the major cities. There were few building restrictions and planning consent and building regulations were still many years in the future.

As the number of houses being built increased, so the prices fell. In the mid 1920s a small bungalow could be bought for £225, a house without a parlour for £350-400, a house with a parlour for £500-600. By the 1930s this had fallen to £450 for a three bedroomed semi-detached property and £775 for a three bedroomed detached in the suburbs of London. In other cities the prices were far lower.

Mortgages became more readily available and building societies started encouraging people on modest salaries to take out a mortgage and buy. The deposit needed to buy fell from 25% of the purchase price in the early twentieth century to just 5% in the late 1920s. Those without savings could still buy a home. This, coupled with fall in interest rates in the 1930s meant that buying became more attractive and repayments more affordable. When building societies started to offer mortgages over 25 year terms, rather than the 15 year terms previously available, repayments fell to 10s per week, far cheaper than renting an equivalent property.

Many of the major builders that we can still see today had their origins in this period. Richard Costain, John Laing, New Ideals Homesteads, Frank Taylor of Taylor Woodrow and George Wimpey.

The peak for private housing was in 1934 when 287,000 new homes were built. This fell to 250,000 in the late 1930s, but it declined almost to zero during the Second World War.

This rush of house building did have its critics. Although the houses were built to a low density (the number of houses per acre of land), there were few local amenities in the suburbs. Schools were built by local authorities for the residential areas, but the spaces left for shops, cinemas, doctor's surgeries and pubs were often left vacant for many years. Commuters, relying on train or tram, would have long, crowded journeys into the centre of the city where they worked. One or two hour commutes were common.

As the 1930s progressed so the intensity and density of building increased. Rooms in the new houses became smaller and the stoves were the solid fuel type that had been so criticised in the past. However, these houses did have their benefits. Coal was still cheaper than gas or electricity, they had electric sockets in almost all rooms and there were airing cupboards, baths, sinks, running hot water, lighting and central heating. And these houses were far easier to keep clean than the old Victorian ones.

Home ownership and the small modern house was here to stay.

2.1.5. Items in the Home

Even before the war there were reports and enquiries into the state of housing in the countryside and the towns and cities. Many were shocked by what was found. Even for those who would have considered themselves above the breadline, the housing was sub-standard. It was not just the homes themselves that were in need of clearance. The items in the home were often in a poor state of repair too.

2.1.6. Pre 1914

The majority of working class families lived on about 20s – 40s (£1 - £2) per week. Labourers might earn a little less, skilled tradesmen a little more. Stonemasons, bricklayers, print workers, warehouseman and other workers who managed to keep their jobs handed the majority of their weekly wages to their wife to allow her to budget for the week. From this she would feed and clothe the family, keep the house clean and tidy and manage the payment of rent each week and buy the necessary fuel. But it can't have been easy for them. The need to find money for a doctor one week would mean that there was less to eat for the rest. And when there wasn't enough to go round something had to give. It was usually the wife who went hungry.

2.1.6.1. Cooking

Most of the women who lived in the slums had one kettle, one frying pan, two saucepans (usually both burned and rather thin). She would know her budget for food and would know how to eke this out to the furthest that it could go. Cooking was done over a small fire, with a small oven or shelves up the side.

2.1.6.2. Furniture

The vast majority of homes during this period had very little furniture. It cost money and there was little left to spend on expensive items such as this.

Even for hard-working, respectable working class families there were more children than there were rooms. A family of eight might live in two or three rooms in a house. Beds were usually made with a straw mattress and whatever bedclothes were available. For a family of 6 or 8 there might only be two beds, with one or two thin blankets to keep them warm. The mother, father, baby and toddler would sleep in one and the older children in a small room with a second bed.

A new-born baby would often have to sleep in the family bed, whatever risks there might be with four or five other people sharing the space, as there was no money for a cot or the bedclothes needed to keep the infant warm. Those lucky enough to be given their own cot might get a banana-crate with a sacking base which cost 1s. A chaff filled mattress cost another 2d and blankets 1s 6d. The total cost of 2s 8d was far beyond the reach of many families where their total income was only 30s per week. So the baby would take its place in the family bed with any older children and often the parents too.

Even in the case of illness (such as measles, whooping cough or diphtheria) or childbirth the arrangements would stay the same. There simply wasn't enough room to change things around. This meant that illnesses went from one child to another (and often to the parents) without any way of stopping it.

For the lucky families who had three or four rooms to live in no one would sleep in the kitchen or living room even if the family was a large one. There was no money for the extra bedding needed. Families were quite used to sleeping three or four to a bed with little privacy or solitude and many saw no need to change the arrangements, even when their situation allowed it.

Other furniture was sparse except in the richest of homes. A table in the living room or kitchen was likely to be small with not enough space for a large family. Even if there was, it is unlikely there were enough chairs for them all to sit down. Children rarely sat at a table for meals except dinner and where there were not enough chairs they would have to stand to eat from their plate. At other times children would be expected to sit on the floor. Newspaper might be used in lieu of a cloth over the table and one plate for each family member would be set round the table. But the food was gone in a flash. A drink of water in a tea cup would follow the meal and one cup would be passed round, refilled for each child.

It is unlikely there would be a wardrobe in the bedroom, just a hook on the back of the door, but it was unlikely to be a problem as there were few clothes to hang. A chest of drawerss might be part of the furniture, but in the poorest of families this would double as the larder. A double bed was the main item of furniture, covered with whatever blankets could be found. If the man worked night shifts the bed could be used by four or five members of the family at all times of the day and night.

On the floor in the kitchen strips of linoleum would be easier on the feet than bare floorboards, but there would never be any carpet. If there was a rug it would be made from clothing that was too ragged or too small to wear any longer. There was often no oven in the kitchen, just a small fire where all cooking was done and water boiled.

Water would be heated in saucepans if there was no copper in the house. For those lucky enough to have a copper in the kitchen it was often in someone else's part of the house and the hot water would have to be carried upstairs to use.

But for all this the homes where the woman was good at budgeting and the man was in regular work would be happy, cheerful places, kept clean and tidy by very hard working women.

Middle class homes had more furniture than this, but rooms would still look a little sparse compared with today's standards. But there would be enough for the family to be comfortable and warm. Above all, homes had to be kept clean, neat and tidy. Before the Great War middle class women often had servants to do the work for them. But the furniture was still heavy, dark and ornate. It was difficult to keep clean and often made the rooms look dark and uninviting.

2.1.6.3. Bath time

Different families had different bathing rituals and routines. But only for the very richest was there a designated bathroom in the house with a copper over the bath to heat the water. For most people this was in the future.

In poorer homes children would be bathed once a week, usually on a Friday or Saturday. A tin bath would be placed in front of the fire and hot water brought up from the water tap and copper. If heated in the kitchen then only very small amounts could be heated at a time. But this was rarely a problem as the bath tub would have been very small, only just big enough for a small child to sit down in. Larger children would have to stand in the tub and clean themselves as best they could.

Children would share the water, with the youngest going first, then one after the other. The older children might get a change of water, but often for those who bathed last the water would be cold and dirty; not very appealing.

The mother generally had a bath in the afternoon when she had time and the older children were at school. She would stand in the bath and make the best of things. The father would go to the public baths when he had time and a spare 2d, or if not then he too would have to make the best of a wash one evening at the end of the week when the children were in bed.

Whatever the routine, it would be very hard work for the mother. It is easy to see why the new homes available after the war, with fitted bathrooms and baths and water piped straight to them, were so appealing to working class women.

2.1.7.   Post 1918

As home ownership grew, people wanted to make their homes comfortable. There was more money to spend on luxuries, and the manufacturers of those luxury items made sure that it was easier than ever before to buy them.

Furniture became lighter and less ornate than it had been in Victorian times. In the 1920s and 1930s Art Deco furniture was in; smooth lines, curves and angles. It was easier to clean and made an impression on anyone who called.

In September 1930 a washing machine was shown for the first time at the International Exhibition of Inventors in London. It worked on a semi-automatic principle and clothes went into a big barrel under two plungers. All the housewife had to do was stand and turn a handle, which moved the plungers and cleaned the clothes in the soapy water. Oh, and fill the barrel with hot water (which had to be heated first), add the soap, rinse, wring and then put the clothes through a mangle. But that was still far easier and less tiring than it had been previously.

It was not long before washing machines were available in the shops. A man could buy one for his wife for between £20 and £40. Alongside them were cookers which could be powered by gas or electricity. These were far cleaner than the solid fuel stoves that had been used previously. They also had glass oven doors so the cook could see what was happening without having to open the door and let out half the heat. It was an innovation.

Another innovation was the vacuum cleaner that worked by electricity. It beat the carpets and rugs in situ without them having to be taken out of the room and hung over a line in the rear yard. These were sold by travelling salesmen calling at homes, who would offer them to the housewife for £10 15s to buy, or they could put 10s down and then pay the rest on the 'never never'. Hire purchase agreements made it easy to buy. They were not a new innovation. Hire purchase had been around for many years, but the difference was that families now had a little more spare money, and the number of items available to buy in this way was increasing.

As more houses were wired for electricity, 75% of all homes by 1939, more electric gadgets were offered for sale. There were portable electric heaters that could be moved from room to room, with gas options available for people who preferred them. It was no longer necessary to have a fire in a bedroom if someone was ill, and it was possible to wake up without ice on the inside of the window. All one needed to do was to turn on the fire for a few minutes before getting out of bed.

The Ideal Home Exhibition in London was first held in 1908 and grew in popularity during the 1920s and 1930s. By 1938 it attracted 600,000 visitors and contained a life sized house featuring hundreds of labour saving devices, furniture, garden furniture and elaborate ways of living. In 1938 it also featured no fewer than 12 gardens, complete with pools, waterfalls and shrubs.

Whilst the very poor remained in their overcrowded homes, the new upper working class and the middle class could begin to take advantage of these new innovations and better housing conditions.

2.2.   Food

The quantity, cost and variation of food changed through the first decades of the twentieth century more than those who welcomed in the first seconds of that century would have imagined possible.

2.2.1.   Pre 1914

By 1900 the British had copied the French habit of serving courses separately. Before that the English tradition was that everything was put on the table at the same time; sweet and savoury. Now people wanted a variety of courses. Richer and more elaborate foods were in demand. For the poor though the staple foods didn't vary. Bread, potatoes and tea, with little meat and even less variety.

During 1901 – 1914 thousands of tons of food were imported to Britain from around the world. Because food was plentiful, prices fell.

Frozen beef, lamb, mutton and pork was being imported from Argentina, Australia, New Zealand and the United States of America (USA). Sugar imports that came from

Australia and the West Indies increased. Cheap tea was imported from Assam and Ceylon. All these made the staple British foods cheaper than ever before.

Virtually all families bulked out their diet with bread. British housewives loved the white loaf, even though they knew that the miller had removed almost all the wheat germ from the grain and so it was less nutritious for the family. In 1909 the Bread Reform League launched a 'standard bread' produced with flour containing 80% wheat germ. But women and families wanted the white loaf and they continued to buy it.

2.2.2. Post 1914

During the war years and up to 1920 food was scarce. German ships blocked the import of food from the Empire and the continent. Markets and shops struggled to fill their shelves with food to feed the population. Farms were working at full stretch, but there was still not enough to go round. Queues formed outside the grocers and some rationing was introduced by the end of the war in 1918. Only the foodstuffs that could be grown or created in Britain were available for sale.

Once the constraints of war were over the consumer society of Britain got back into full swing, although food prices were still very high. But even through the terrible years of depression in the 1920s those with money could buy food. Poorer families, and those where the wage earner had lost his job, couldn't afford the food that was available, and the high prices hit even middle class families. Everyone had to spend a greater proportion of their income on the basic foodstuffs and although there was plenty of food available the high cost meant that thousands were now going hungry. It was not until the mid 1930s that wages had increased and unemployment had fallen. Food was affordable again.

Between 1913 and 1934 there was an 88% rise in consumption of fruit, 65% rise in the consumption of vegetables, 46% rise in eggs and 55% rise in fresh milk. However, the consumption of potatoes remained stable and that of bread declined. People were turning away from the staple foods and were spending their money on the cheaper variety of food available.

Imports of tea rose from £336 million in 1918 to £994 million in 1919 and Brook Bond established new plantations in Kenya and Nyasaland in the 1920s. The 7lbs of tea consumed per head in 1914 rose to 9lbs in 1926, aided at least in part by falling prices.

Consumption of fresh milk increased. In the early 1900s each person drank an average of 1.8 pints per week. This increased to an average of 2.8 pints by 1937. This was in spite of the fact that the poor generally avoided fresh milk as it was expensive and didn't keep for long. They didn't have expensive refrigerators and couldn't afford the ice needed for the cool boxes seen in wealthy homes. The poor generally preferred tinned condensed milk. It was full of sugars, which satisfied the sweet tooth developing in Britain, but lasted well. After 1922 all milk was pasteurised to prevent the spread of Tuberculosis. In an effort to stabilise prices the Milk Marketing Board was created to regulate the quality and price of milk delivered to shops and the public.

But the very poor didn't have the money even for the cheaper food available. They waited until the end of market day, then scavenged around the stalls, picking up the food dropped or discarded as unfit for sale. Those with a little money would buy the almost stale bread from the baker or the broken biscuits and vegetables that no one else wanted from the grocer.

2.2.3. Meals

By the twentieth century most people ate three meals a day, much as we do now, although the time of those meals varied greatly depending on the family's class and means.

2.2.3.1. Breakfast

A housewife on a small budget was more likely to cook food that both her husband and children would eat, rather than that which was best for them. Food such as porridge, which was nutritious and healthy, was rarely eaten for breakfast because men and children didn't like it. There was never any fresh milk or sugar to tempt the children as these were expensive and not things the housewife would buy. Also porridge took a long time to cook so needed expensive fuel for the fire and someone to stir it when the housewife was busy trying to get the children ready for school. Breakfast would be a slice of bread and margarine with a sip of weak tea. This had to sustain a person for their morning's work, whether that was school or hard labour.

For the better off breakfast was a meal eaten very early before work, but they had their choice of what to eat; toast and butter, jams or fish.

2.2.3.2. Lunch

Lunch had little place in working class society during the first decades of the twentieth century although it was now common in upper class households. The term was first used in the 1830s when 'luncheon' was a small meal taken between two more substantial ones, but it could be eaten at any time of the day. It was only during the 1920s that the name was gradually given to the small meal that ladies, and it was exclusively ladies, ate at midday or early afternoon.

Mrs Beeton's Book of Household Management (1861) stated that it should be eaten 'between early breakfast and late dinner...A healthy person with good exercise should have a fresh supply of food once in four hours....' But she goes on to state that the amount eaten should be proportionate to the length of time the lady would have to wait for dinner. Clearly rumbling stomachs were not acceptable in society!

For the better off lunch would be a leisurely affair, either eaten with friends or alone. Although servants were less common after 1920 middle class women could take advantage of the new labour saving devices available and they still had more time for a leisurely meal and become 'ladies that lunch'.

2.2.3.3. Dinner

This was the main meal of the day, most often eaten at midday although in working class households everyone was likely to eat separately during the working week. The children would be fed their dinner when they got home from school in the middle of the day, sitting or standing at a table in the kitchen. They would have their own plate, but cutlery was rare.

The husband would eat when he returned from work, often quite late in the evening. The best of the meat and food would be saved for him, in recognition that he needed his strength as the wage earner. If there was little food or money then it was the wife who went without. Where economies had to be made she made them in her own meal. After all, she didn't have to go out to work and the children were expected to be attentive at school and she made sure that they had the best she could offer.

The meal would usually consist of potatoes, vegetables and a little meat if it was available. 4lbs of flank beef would feed a family of six for three days and provide dinner for the man of the house during the working week. It would be stewed with vegetables to get the most from it. Children would be given very little of the meat, just a small cube with gravy. Bones and fat would all be used for stock. There was so little to go round that there could be no wastage.

For those better off the children would be sat at a table, either in the dining room or kitchen, where they would eat meat, vegetables and have a drink of water or mild ale.

2.2.3.4. Supper

This was a light meal eaten late at night, usually by the higher classes, either whilst out visiting friends at balls and parties, or shortly before retiring to bed.

It was unlikely to be eaten by the working class. There was often little enough to go round and so children, men and women alike would often go to bed hungry.

3. Out and About

3.1. Shopping

Shopping has been a necessity since people ceased to be self-sufficient. By 1901 towns and cities had developed a multitude of shops catering for everything from foodstuffs, to clothes and the luxuries that people were willing to pay for. If there was a market for it, then someone found a way to either manufacture it, grow it or import it. The ports of England and Wales brought in thousands of tons of goods every year which were transported to the shops, either by road, rail or canal. The years 1901 to 1939 saw the biggest transformations in shopping habit not repeated until the online market developed in the early twenty first century.

At the start of the twentieth century towns and cities were serviced by a multitude of small shops owned and run by families who needed to make a living. They were specialists in making sure that they provided what people wanted to buy, happy to provide the expertise and advice people needed.

In order to shop women, with their young children in tow, would go from grocer to baker, from stationer to haberdashery, choosing the items they needed and hauling them home in their baskets. Some of the local stores, particularly the grocers, would arrange a home delivery service for their regular customers, especially those who could afford to pay.

By 1901 the consumer society was well underway. Many traders had their own premises, most of which had living accommodation above. There were large glass windows displaying their wares to entice the buyers. Huge canvas awnings and painted signs told the customer what goods or services the shop sold. A red and white pole indicated a barber, three gold coloured balls were the sign of a pawnbroker. They were there as an advertisement. Displays spread onto the pavements and tempting smells from the bakery would drift along the street.

Markets were still in evidence, often once or twice a week. The noisy traders shouted their prices, each vying to outdo the other. Colourful materials, ribbons and bonnets would dance in the wind and bright, fresh vegetables laid out in boxes tempting women to part with their pennies and shillings.

But even by 1901 things were changing, particularly in the cities and larger towns. Shops were getting bigger, selling a wider variety of goods under one roof. The Cooperative movement, started in the 1860s in the north of England, was expanding. Their shops sold both food and non-foodstuffs. By 1914 they had three million members and shops across the country with a turnover of £80 million; their greatest numbers in working class areas. Women wanted to be able to buy different goods in the same place. They didn't want to spend time trawling round the streets looking for the things they wanted. They wanted convenience.

In 1914 the working class family spent three quarters of its income on food and housing. In 1938 this had fallen to under one half of their income. The money they had left at the end of the week paid for luxuries that they couldn't have afforded before; Tobacco (consumption of which multiplied five times by 1939), clothing and items for the house. By 1939 two out of every three houses were wired for electricity. Status was no longer measured by whether you could keep a servant but on the number of domestic gadgets that the home had: radios, washing machines, electric cookers and vacuum cleaners.

In 1901 2.5% of total consumer expenditure went on furniture, electric goods and motor cars. By 1938 this had risen to nearly 6%. Shopkeepers enticed women to spend their extra cash in their stores; they were quick to see the possibilities.

Montague Burton started in 1905 as a general outfitter. In 1914 he had five stores in the north of England, but by 1919 this had increased to 40 shops, half of them in London. By 1929 this had grown to 400 shops, together with mills and factories. In 1939 the chain had grown to 565 shops with over 90% of them outside London; there would have been one on almost every High Street in sizable towns in England and Wales.

In 1921 the man about town would go to his local Montague Burton store, choose a style from their catalogue, the fabric from a swatch and place his order, paying a small deposit. He would collect the suit a week later. During the 1930s ready-to-wear, off the peg suits took over from tailor made and Burton's shops adapted to deal with this change. Teachers, shop assistants and clerks all wore suits to work, some shabbier and older than others. Burton made sure that the company could cater for the masses.

In 1935 Good Housekeeping magazine reported that a typical female town dweller would spend £15 1s 3d per year on cleaning cream, powder, lipstick, rouge, 2 permanent waves, fortnightly shampoo and set, plus manicures three times each year. For a typist in a provincial town it was more likely to be £3 2s 2d. However, whatever the total amount spent it was clear that thousands of women across the country could afford to spend money on themselves and were prepared to do so. There were hairdressers' shops, clothing and makeup manufacturers with shops to display their merchandise. Women wanted to make the best of their appearance. Dressing smartly was no longer just for the wealthy.

For the poor the picture wasn't quite so rosy. Not everyone had more money in their pockets to spend on themselves. For many it was still a struggle to feed the family and keep a roof over their heads. They had no money for new clothes or make up. They got their clothes from friends and relations who no longer used them. They might buy second-hand from markets or local rag man. Long before the age of recycling and charity shops, our ancestors were wearing second-hand clothes out of necessity.

Second-hand clothes were not only worn by the poor. Those who liked to wear more expensive clothes than their income allowed might respond to advertisements in *The Lady*, placed by a "widow in reduced circumstances", or "a titled lady" who was selling off part of her wardrobe. There were also dress agencies that advertised in *The Lady* and other periodicals. They usually had discrete premises in good areas of the town or city, often on the first floor, where their customers would not be seen buying second-hand clothes.

The advent of ready to wear clothes meant that prices fell and many more people could afford to wear new and fashionable clothes. In 1901 most shops were small, where the shopper would be greeted by a salesman, or increasingly a woman, who would bring the goods to the shopper to examine. The arrival of new, much larger department stores, selling a multitude of items to tempt the shopper, changed all that.

Co-Operative stores were expanding in the north of the country and by 1938 they sold one third of all women and children's clothes. Woolworth's first store opened in Liverpool in 1909. Originally selling only items priced between 3d and 6d, they were cheap and advertised widely, spreading throughout the country very quickly. Marks and Spencer were another store that soon dominated the High Street. They rebuilt and extended many of their stores in the 1920s, taking advantage of the ready-to-wear market. By 1939 they had 234 stores and employed 17,000 people. Originally selling hardware, cutlery, china, toys, haberdashery and confectionery they moved into clothes during the 1930s as the distinction between lower and middle class clothes had largely disappeared. Initially they aimed at the working class market, the move towards a middle class clientele coming much later in the century.

By 1901 W H Smiths were already a household name, selling stationary and books and in 1903 they opened their first overseas shop. Originally they only had stores at railway stations, but they moved to High Street stores after a disagreement lost them some prime railway station locations. They expanded rapidly after that.

Other stores that flourished in the 1930s were Lipton's, His Master's Voice gramophone record store and Dewhursts the Butchers. C&A arrived from the Netherlands in the 1920s and claimed their place on the High Street. Home and Colonial Stores merged with the Lipton's supermarket chain (which started as one shop in Glasgow in 1881) in 1929 to form a group with 3,000 stores nationwide.

London, saw the rise of some very large department stores that stayed in the city and didn't spread across the country. Each large department store would vie to outdo the others in the city. Kennards hired three baby elephants for their "Jumbo Sale" in 1930. Bentalls displayed Malcolm Campbell's Bluebird car which had just broken the land speed record. Selfridges, which opened in 1909 and had become the UK's second largest shop by the 1930s, opened a roof garden in 1930, having had it designed to entice Londoners out into the sunshine in the hope that they would spend their shillings on the way back down to the street. Derry and Tom's roof garden (1938) comprised a Spanish, Tudor and English woodland; one and a half acres of roof top space.

By the 1930s small, independent stores were being squeezed out. They depended upon first-hand knowledge and the personality of the proprietor, but people were drawn by the dazzling array of goods, all displayed behind plate glass windows, with well-dressed shop assistants ready to serve. In department stores the goods were on display for shoppers to touch and comment on to one another, not hidden in drawers behind the counter that only the shop keeper could reach. Shopping habits were changing. Shops had to either change with them, or they quickly went out of business. Unfortunately for many of the smaller shops, they went the latter way.

3.2. Transport

As the new Edwardian era dawned the Population of England and Wales was growing and the methods of transport changed. The large number of people needing work and housing meant that they couldn't all live in the centre of the rapidly growing urban areas. Indeed for the wealthy it was far from desirable to live near the poor and unwashed rabble that comprised the majority of the population. They wanted to set themselves apart from the masses.

In turn the move away from the city centres affected the working- and middle-class too. Cheap, reliable transport became essential.

3.2.1. Canals

In 1901 canals transported large amounts of cargo up and down the country, although the passengers they had once carried had largely been transferred to the railways by this time. At the start of the twentieth century engines were being fitted to the colourful canal boats that trawled up and down the country on narrow strips of water. Until then they had been towed by horses, which were regular and dependable, but needed caring for and stabling overnight.

Fig 3.1: Horse drawn canal boat on the Grand Western Canal, Devon.

Canal boats were also very slow. News and perishable goods needed to reach their destination quickly and railways were ideal. Another drawback was that in winter the canals often froze, effectively making them useless for weeks at a time. But for bulky or fragile goods the canals were still popular.

Up until 1939 canals were still in regular use for the transportation of goods from one major city to another, but the railways were taking over as the railway network could carry freight much further than the canals had ever been able to.

3.2.2. Railways

Railways started their march across the country in the Victorian era, and by the start of Edward's reign there were over 18,500 miles of track, 1,100 million passengers and millions of tons of freight were carried by rail each year. Imported goods were brought to the ports and the railways carried them to their destinations.

Letters were carried for the Post Office, enabling fast and efficient carriage of mail to all areas of England and Wales. Perishable food and newspapers could also be delivered quickly and efficiently. London newspapers would leave the city late at night and would be in Cardiff in time for the early editions to go on sale the next day.

Fig 3.2: Steam engines were a popular and common form of transport in the early 20th Century. 4160 steaming through the Somerset countryside.

Railways allowed people to travel quickly and cheaply between towns and cities. People could now travel 20 miles to adjacent markets, or for entertainment, and so the 'pool' of friends became much larger. Journeys across the country could be completed in a few hours, whereas previously they would have taken several days. In 1938 the *Mallard* became the fastest steam engine in the world at 126 miles per hour. By the start of the twentieth century it was a quick and comfortable way to travel.

But for passengers railways were expensive and not economical over distances of less than ten miles. Only London was of a size to benefit from this sort of transport. In other, smaller towns and cities, such as Bristol, Birmingham and Leeds, most people couldn't afford to commute by railway. For many a journey by rail would have been something exciting (or terrifying) and different. Not something undertaken every day.

3.2.3.   Electric Trams and Trolleybuses

Electric trams started to make an appearance in the 1890s. The total length of track in Britain grew from just 1,000 miles in 1900 to over 2,500 miles by 1911. These were 40% cheaper to run than horse drawn trams. The fares gradually fell and these became a realistic means of travel from the outskirts of a town or city to the centre, either for work, for shopping expeditions or for entertainment.

The electric tram had a short lived popularity. The track was inflexible and expensive to set down and by the 1930s local authorities were replacing them with trolleybuses. These were trams which no longer needed to run on a track, but took their power from overhead live electricity wires that stretched along the route. Leeds and Bradford were the first cities to use trolleybuses in 1911. By 1938 Birmingham was operating 1,224 Midland Red trolleybuses and most of the larger cities had networks operating on their main streets.

For those living in larger towns and cities these would have been a common sight. They would have paid the cheap fare, of 1d or 2d, and climbed aboard. They would have looked much like the older buses on the streets today, but sparks would fly where the wheel and cable that powered the bus met the overhead electricity cable. The buses were almost silent, running on rubber tires and moving quickly through the streets of the towns. Accidents were common, where a pedestrian had walked out in front of the bus because they hadn't hear it coming.

3.2.4. Busses

After the First World War the diesel combustion engine became more popular. Buses no longer needed the expensive wires that predetermined the routes and trams and trolley busses gradually fell out of use. The motor bus was especially popular for out of town routes, bringing people into the town's centre for work and shopping. Some men who had learned to drive as soldiers during the war took their war gratuities, bought cheap second hand vehicles and set themselves up in business. In the early 1920s 80% of bus operators owned fewer than five vehicles.

In rural areas passengers were often carried in open top lorries with bench seats - especially for working class outings. At other times the same lorries would be used to transport freight. The 1920s saw a rapid expansion of motor buses. Regular services in rural areas and improvements in pneumatic tyres brought the first luxury, long distance routes and regular Greyhound service commenced between Bristol and London. By 1939 53,000 buses and coaches were operating in Great Britain.

3.2.5. Lorries

With the improvement in roads and the development of the combustion engine, goods were more frequently transported by road. In 1905 there were 4,000 goods vehicles on the road which had increased to 82,000 by 1914. Numbers rose quickly after the war, to nearly 500,000 by 1939. And the first motorway was still 15 years away. Roads through towns and villages were getting busier and more people were getting killed or injured in accidents. Quiet country lanes were a thing of the past.

3.2.6. Motor Cars

There were two other inventions that affected transport during this period. The first was the motor car. Invented in 1880s it was the Motor Car Act of 1903 that allowed them to travel at speeds of up to 20 miles per hour (the man with the red flag no longer required). There were just 8,000 on the roads in 1904, but by 1914 this had risen to 132,000. However, with a total population of over 36 million it is clear that only a very few wealthy individuals had access to, or even saw, the motor car.

At first it was professional men, such as doctors and lawyers, who owned motor cars. The Vauxhall Motor Company started in 1903 and the first Rolls Royce Silver Shadow was produced in 1906. Herbert Austin started the production of small cars at his Longbridge factory in 1910, the same year that Henry Ford set up his factory at Trafford Park, Manchester.

In spite of the 1903 Act by the early 1920s some cars were able to exceed 100 miles per hour. In 1930 the maximum speed limit was set at 30 miles per hour in urban areas, with no maximum speed on the open roads and this was not changed until the 1960s. In 1926 the world land speed record was set by Malcolm Campbell's *Bluebird* at just over 300 miles per hour.

After the First World War the number of cars on the road grew rapidly. In 1920 there were 187,000 in use, rising to over two million by 1939. It is estimated that there were over a hundred private cars for every mile of classified road in the country. Most people didn't have cars, or even have access to them, but by 1939 they were a common sight on Britain's roads.

3.2.7. Bicycles

The second innovation that affected large numbers of the population was the bicycle. By 1900 a rear-chain-driven bicycle with pneumatic tyres was being mass produced and it became a popular form of transport during the early 1900s. Without it most people would have had to either use public transport or, more likely, walk. They were hugely popular amongst the young and less well off. Many early motor car firms started out as bicycle manufactures.

Motor bikes quickly developed from the popularity of bicycles and it was not until the mid 1920s that the numbers of motor cars overtook the number of motor bicycles on the roads (half a million).

3.2.8. Air Transport

But for all the transport that existed around this small island, to leave Great Britain the only realistic way was by sea. Air travel was still very much in its infancy. The first powered flight took place on 17th December 1903 and lasted 59 seconds, Wilbur Wright flew 852 feet (260 meters) and that was just the start. In 1909 Bleriot made the first flight across the channel and the first scheduled passenger flight from London to Paris started in 1919.

Although air travel had its roots during the 1920s and 1930s, it wasn't in use for even the wealthiest of people until the 1940s and beyond.

3.2.9. Steam Ships

Longer journeys took place by steam ship. Large liners were being built in the huge ship building centres in this country and in Ireland. Ships were becoming larger and more luxurious, carrying people to new lives in America and Australia. They catered for those able to pay large sums for comfort and luxury, whilst the poorer classes were crammed on lower decks, squeezed into large dormitory style cabins and less salubrious places. The shipping lines catered for them all.

The *Titanic* and her sister ship the *Olympic,* were the height in luxury and heralded the ultimate in style and comfort for those who wished to travel. But they were also the last of their kind. From the 1920s onward people were more interested in travelling quickly rather than taking their time to get anywhere. As air flight became possible for the mainstream population the popularity of sea travel diminished for many years.

Throughout the first decades of the twentieth century large volumes of freight travelled by sea, both imports and exports. It was Britain's link to the world.

3.3. Sport

The need for fresh air and exercise to promote healthy bodies was recognised long before the start of the twentieth century. At the end of the nineteenth century there was a push for public parks and open green spaces in towns and cities that could be used by families for walking and general exercise. Before this time there had only been private green areas that the poor and middle classes were not permitted to use.

The sports that men and women took part in were little different than those that had been enjoyed in the eighteenth and nineteenth centuries. The main difference was that many working class people now had the time and energy to take part. Most workers had a half day off at the weekend, Saturday afternoon, which was likely to be used for sport.

For urban working class men cricket, bowls, billiards and athletics were all popular. There were often facilities attached to a public house or to works clubs set up by large employers. In the country cricket was often played on the village green, often the teams being the wealthier men of the area known as the 'gentlemen' and the lower classes, known as the 'players'.

Women generally were less involved in sports. Working class women still had less leisure time, although as the century progressed the labour saving devices that gradually appeared in homes did help matters. Those that did take part were generally young, unmarried women.

Tennis and golf were both middle class sports. Golf started in Scotland and clubs only gradually opened in England and Wales. Working class men were not encouraged on the greens and high club membership fees were charged to effectively keep them out.

During the early twentieth century football was the 'peoples' game. It was usually unorganised and rowdy until 1863 when rules for the game were set down and the Football Association formed. With the arrival of Saturday afternoons off work, football became a very popular past time; either playing or watching it.

In 1880 Birmingham had 344 football clubs, 83 having religious affiliations. Liverpool in 1885 had 112, with 25 being religious. Professional players were allowed from 1885, although usually only part time. They were paid as much as a skilled artisan, £30 - 40 per week. Transfer fees could be as high as £1,000 in 1905. The money for the teams came from local businesses and politicians. Before 1963 there was a maximum wage fixed, which kept the salaries in line with the average salary. As football became more popular and players became paid to play many of those town and city clubs turned professional. Watching the game became more popular as the years went by.

The first English Football Association Cup Final was played in London in 1895 in front of 45,000 spectators. By 1913 the crowd was 120,000 and it was very big business.

Rugby followed a different course. The Rugby Union was formed in 1871 and all players were amateurs which dominated until 1895. Working class players needed to fund their playing as they didn't get paid enough to only work part time and broke away to form the Rugby League. The Rugby Union continued to only permit amateur players until late in the twentieth century.

Women were greatly restricted in sports by the clothes they wore. From the nineteenth century they played croquet, tennis, golf (although ladies were only permitted to play a full round of golf after 1885) but their movement was greatly hindered. The first Wimbledon singles final was played in 1886.

Some women tried to dress differently, wearing bloomers under their skirts or wearing cycling shorts, but they were harshly criticised for doing so. But after the First World War, by which time their clothing was generally simpler, it became more acceptable for them to wear trousers or even short skirts.

Amateur sport was very popular, particularly as Saturdays became accepted as a day off. Amateur leagues for cricket, football, rugby and other sports were played between towns and villages close enough to travel to one another's grounds for the day. Great pride, and not some small amount of time, was put into practice and competitions. Photographs of these teams can be found in the local newspapers dating back to the early twentieth century.

3.4.   Entertainment

By 1939 the British pub, which had been a staple part of entertainment for British men for hundreds of years, was declining in popularity. It was being replaced by working men's clubs, drinking at football matches and at the cinema and numerous other attractions. There was a greater choice of entertainment than ever before.

3.4.1.   Music Hall

Music Hall and palaces of varieties were a major source of public entertainment from the middle of the nineteenth century and up to the First World War. The small establishments of the early years were amalgamated into larger premises by the start of the Great War. By 1914 the capital investment in London's major music halls was estimated at £5 million, although ownership was held by just a few companies.

London's success spread out to the provinces. As it did so the general tone of the entertainment was modified. There was too much money invested to risk offending the paying audiences and the music halls of the twentieth century became much tamer than those of earlier times. Coarseness, eating, drinking and often smoking were banned in cheaper seats. Productions were turned into cosy, romanticised presentations.

3.4.2.   Picture Houses

At the start of the century a new form of entertainment vied for the public's money. The first public showing of a film took place in London in 1896. These silent movies were much more realistic than the old magic lantern shows and people loved them. Their popularity spread rapidly. Initially showings took place in music halls, but purpose built picture theatres, palaces and houses soon appeared, the word 'cinema' first being used in 1910. By 1915 Birmingham had at least 57 cinemas and it is estimated that there were approximately 3,000 in the country as a whole.

These early films were silent, with captions telling the story and actors miming their parts. 'Talkies' followed in 1929, and although Charlie Chaplin dismissed them as rubbish that would soon disappear, they soon became even more popular than silent movies. The first colour film was shown in the 1930s.

By 1917 it was estimated that over half the population went to the cinema at least once each week. In 1939 the cheapest seats were 6d, well within the reach of the majority of the population, although there were still many who could not afford it.

Audiences increased. Buildings that had been built just a decade before could no longer seat all the people who wanted to see the films. Grander, bigger cinemas were built in a variety of styles. The grand 1930s Art Deco buildings became an icon of the era. They were aimed at middle class as well as working class folk. Large chains appeared, such as Gaumont and British Internationals, then Oscar Deutsch's Odeon.

By 1939 even a mid-sized city such as York had 10 cinemas and an estimated weekly audience of 50,000. One half of the attendees were children and of the rest, three quarters were women.

The cinema had become a part of everyday life, along with Hollywood and British stars, glamorous productions and the darkness of the back row.

By 1939 it is estimated that there were 5,000 cinemas in Britain, with weekly audiences of 30 million. Pathe News reels brought moving pictures of big news events, just as television does today.

3.4.3.   Theatre

In spite of the huge growth in the popularity of the cinema, it did not take all the business away from live theatre, which remained popular. The theatre of the time was dominated by George Bernard Shaw, J M Barrie and John Galsworthy, with the light comedy and musicals of Noel Coward.

Theatres also produced local repertory companies following the example of Annie Hornioman at Manchester Gaiety Theatre in 1908. Gallery prices were 4d and the pit was 9d. The prices compared very favourably with those of the cinema and music hall.

3.4.4.   Dance Halls

As the twentieth century progressed dance halls also became popular. They appealed to the young and it was a place where courting couples would go.

Churches often held dances, believing that young courting couples could attend without any worry that things would get out of hand. In larger cities, town halls would hold dances with live bands, popular with working- and middle-class couples alike. The old fashioned waltzes were replaced by the foxtrot, tango and the Charleston, which came over with the Americans during the war.

New music forms came with the Americans too. Jazz in the form of Ragtime and Blues and the big band swing of the 1930s changed the dance halls forever.

3.4.5. Gramophones

It was not only at the cinemas and dance halls where the new music trends could be heard. The gramophone could bring stars such as George Formby, Harry Lauder and Gracie Fields to the front room. Gramophone records could be brought and shared by anyone with a love of music.

Prices were realistic and gramophones were one of the many new items that benefitted from electricity and the spread of buying on credit. Now music could fill the front room of even modest houses at the rattle of the needle.

3.4.6. Radio

The first radio broadcasts were made in 1922. The British Broadcasting Corporation, a state run organisation, was set up in 1926 and had a statutory monopoly in Britain. The number of annual licences issued (at a cost of 10s each) increased from 35,744 in 1922 to over two million by the time the BBC was set up in 1926. In 1939 over nine million licences were sold. A radio could be brought for £1 and were very popular with almost everyone.

There were a variety of programs broadcast by the BBC. Some were news programs and others light music. But the new radios could also pick up broadcasts from commercial companies abroad, Radio Luxembourg being one of them. They broadcast a much greater variety of music and short serialised stories, often sponsored by soap manufacturers, which became known as 'soap operas'.

3.5. Hobbies

Hobbies became more popular during the early twentieth century. With a growing amount of money to spend on themselves people were developing leisure interests that would keep them occupied.

For many this was gardening in the yard at the back of the house they had bought. Stamp collecting became popular at this time as did the new hobby of photography.

The Box Brownie had been developed by Eastman Kodak in America and was soon being sold in the shops in towns and cities all over Britain. It utilised strips of coated plastic film in place of heavy glass plates of yesteryear. The early cameras came pre-loaded with film and the user would simply send the whole camera back to the shop for development. The printed photographs, in glorious black and white, could be collected some days later.

As time went on the cameras became more usable, with collapsible bellows allowing the whole camera to be easily slipped into a pocket. The back could be removed allowing for the film to be changed by the user, so that only the film had to be sent back for processing. The camera owner could use as much film as he wanted in a single outing.

For a guide as to the number of hobbies that were becoming popular it is only necessary to look and see how many magazines began during this time (see Section 6.5).

Fig 3.3: 1914 Kodak Camera.

3.6. Holidays

Looking at census returns at ten year periods (and usually for March or April dates) it is difficult to catch times when our forebears were on holiday. However, in the early twentieth century holidays were becoming increasingly popular as people started to acquire a higher standard of living and paid holidays from work made their appearance.

The official modern definition of "holiday" is four or more nights away from home. This was rarely possible for lower middle class or working class families until holidays with pay were introduced, although some employers, churches, chapels, Sunday schools and friendly societies tried to take working class children away for a day at the seaside each year. North West Railway Company workers received holiday with pay by 1914, but this was the exception rather than the rule.

In 1901 20,000 quarter fare tickets were sold for the annual holiday Wakes Week in Crewe. Most went to Blackpool, but there were many who went to the Isle of Man, the North Wales coast or Scotland, Ireland or the continent. The majority of these would have been those who were wealthy enough to spend time away. The poor would remain at home and enjoy a break, if they could afford it, away from the toil of the factories or farms.

The pattern of Public Holidays remained much as it had been in the nineteenth century. The number of official holidays had been reduced in 1808 from 44 to just 4 (Christmas, Good Friday, 1 May and 1 November). An 1871 Act provided four further public holidays at Boxing Day, Easter Monday, Whit Monday and the first Monday in August. Employees in manufacturing areas, mainly in the north of England and North Wales, would take a Wakes Week, with or without authority from their employers. However, it was not long before the employers realised the benefit of closing their factories for a week so they could arrange for maintenance to be carried out at a time when they were not paying their workforce to stand idly by. They generally closed for a week at each of Whitsun, Christmas and early autumn.

Because of the extra time away from work the "day away" of the early twentieth century grew to a weekend and then a full week away from home for those who could afford it. Gradually the traditional calendar rearranged itself around these dates. An August holiday was established in the first week of August, except where a later Wakes Week was taken. This pattern continued until the 1950s, except during the first and second world wars. Gradually holidays became more frequent and longer.

The wealthy either went abroad, to Torquay or Sidmouth in the South West of England, or St Andrews in Scotland. The comfortably off generally spent a week at a small hotel in Tynemouth, Llandudno or Bournemouth. The upper working class might have a few days at Blackpool, Hunstanton or Margate depending upon where they lived. The very poor would not have any time away and even a Wakes Week would cause them terrible hardship, when they would have to seek some form of alternative employment for a short time, such as hop picking in the Kent countryside.

By 1937 about three million workers had some holidays with pay. However the Holidays with Pay Act of 1938 added another 11 million to this figure and the holiday was here to stay.

Billy Butlin opened his first holiday camp in Skegness in 1937. Clacton opened in 1939, by which time there were 200 other smaller holiday camps in Britain attracting 30,000 visitors per week in peak season. It cost £1 per day of entertainment at Butlin's and attracted large numbers of lower middle class people. However, he failed to capture the working class trade as this type of holiday remained out of their reach.

The other big change to life at this time was the emergence of the weekend. Initially people only had a half day off on Sunday, but gradually this changed and Sunday became a day of rest. Saturday was a half day holiday for most people and it stretched to become a day when they played or watched sport, enjoyed a hobby or spent time with the family.

3.7.   Migration, Emigration and Immigration

3.7.1.   Migration

During the first half of the twentieth century there were three main patterns of migration within the country.

People moved from small settlements to larger settlements, often from rural areas to urban area or from outlying region to more central area. This was largely a continuation of the pattern that started in the nineteenth century. Generally people moved to a place where there was work.

As the older industrial centres declined people moved away to find new work elsewhere. Skills from the old industries were not easily transferred to any new industry in an area and so people often moved some distance to find work that they were skilled to do. Skilled work paid higher wages and that made it worth uprooting the family and taking them to a previously unknown area.

With improvements to transport, especially with the arrival of the car, people moved from towns to the countryside in areas of employment and growth. People became more mobile. They could commute to their place of work and would move their families out to healthier and more pleasant places to live. There were also slum clearance schemes in city centres which forced people to move when they might not otherwise have afforded to, or wanted to do.

In the early 1900s the restrictions to a right to poor relief still applied. In England and Wales someone needed to have been born in the parish, have married someone from the parish or have lived and worked in the parish and acquired their right through that work. Any person who became a burden on the poor rates could be removed within 40 days from an area where they had no right of settlement.

This could restrict mobility of labour, particularly where areas suffered a decline in employment because of declining industries or failure of crops, although the surveys carried out suggest that it wasn't a serious obstacle to mobility. Our ancestors seem to have been largely optimistic when it came to needing to move for work. The removal of paupers was expensive for a parish and areas that needed workers would generally welcome them. The alternative to removal was often payment of costs incurred in temporary relief by the parish on which the rate charge fell, rather than accepting the paupers back to the parish.

Families might also have been reluctant to move for personal, family or community reasons. Often things would have to get very bad for people to move away. Major reasons were the collapse in local employment, i.e. mills going out of business, changes in local landholding, or simply the pressure of overpopulation and decay of rural industry.

In the early twentieth century the government implemented local policies to try to boost employment in decaying regions. They provided grants to set up new industry and train workers. The war also boosted employment, almost eliminating unemployment altogether. This meant that for many people who had been out of work for months, or even years, companies were prepared to train them or they could enlist in one of the forces.

3.7.2. Emigration

Migration overseas might have been the movement of choice for some, but for many it would have been the last resort. Many of the poorest in the country couldn't afford to go unless there was financial help available. Some churches paid the cost of the passage abroad for some, or the Government paid for orphaned children to be sent to countries in the Empire, such as Canada.

Many simply went for a better life for themselves and their families. Land was cheaper and, where they couldn't have started their own business in this country, there were opportunities and possibilities for them abroad.

In 1901 levels of emigration were higher than ever before. The majority were going to countries of the Empire, especially Canada, Australia, South Africa and to the British North America.

In 1911 455,000 left British ports for countries outside Europe. 29% left for the USA, 41% for Canada, 18% for Australia and 7% for South Africa. For many the First World War brought their dreams to a premature end, causing them to enlist for the British Overseas Forces and return to Europe to fight.

By the 1930s the volume of emigration had fallen to levels not seen since the 1870s, with those few who were leaving favouring Australia and Canada. During that decade there were more people coming into the Britain from America and the 'White Commonwealth' than those leaving for those countries. The world had changed.

3.7.3.   Immigration

The Aliens Act of 1905 and the Aliens Restrictions Act 1919 made Britain a far less open country than it had been in the nineteenth century. However, political problems in Europe ensured many refugees still came to Britain; Jews, Poles, Ukrainians and Hungarians all faced German advancements in the 1930s. But the numbers were small.

There were three other groups of people who came to Britain hoping for a better life for themselves.

The Irish. These came from Ulster and the South. By the twentieth century the flood of Irish immigrants had diminished to a trickle. Only about 10,000 arrived in 1911. However, those who did come were extremely poor and had something of a reputation, whether or not earned, of drinking and fighting. The stereotypical image was difficult for them to leave behind and they suffered severe prejudice.

The Jews. These came mainly from Eastern Europe. Again, there were not huge numbers in the twentieth century, but most came because of persecution abroad. They worked here as pedlars and street traders, as they had been before they arrived, but they incurred the resentment of London Costermongers and others who plied their trade in the same way. Only a few established shops and those who did were in major areas of Jewish immigration. They tended to stay together, such as in the east end of London, Strangeways and West Bank of Manchester. The streets where they lived were generally 80% Jewish and the natives of the city felt that they were establishing ghettos. Like the Irish they sank to the bottom of the labour market, but they would work for the lowest terms rather than be unemployed. They always worked to improve themselves and the areas they lived in. In 1901 there were 50 synagogues in Britain, and by 1950 there were 240.

Coloured/Blacks. Most of the major sea ports had a significant number of black immigrants. In 1901 Cardiff had about 700 Africans and West Indians. They arrived on ships from the Africas but once they had left their ships they found it difficult to find another to take them on. They were very poor, predominantly male and found it very difficult to find work. At the start of the First World War they were taken on as the demand for labour and soldiers was high and it transformed their economic situation. However, at the end of the war demobilisation increased Liverpool's coloured population from 2,000 to 5,000 and Cardiff's from 700 to 3,000. They were poor, unemployed and unlikely to find work because of local prejudice. 600 accepted voluntary repatriation between 1918 and 1920. They were in an impossible situation. Whilst they had British citizenship they were treated as Aliens under the Acts of 1905 and 1919.

4.   Children

The general mantra of the Victorians, that 'children should be seen but not heard', still held at the start of the twentieth century. But as time went on more people recognised that children were people in their own right and that they needed protection.

By 1870 all children under ten were required to attend school and in 1874 it became illegal to employ children under ten full time. The state recognised that it was important that children should receive some form of education and the amount required increased as the twentieth century progressed.

Children were believed to be intrinsically evil, that they needed harsh treatment and strict discipline to ensure that they learned how to become valuable and honest members of society. This was how their parents had been brought up and now it was their turn. Their parents needed them to get out to work as quickly as possible to bring in a much needed income. Education was generally despised, because it was seen to give children ideas above their station and it stopped them working as soon as they were able to. The belief was that they should be educated to their station in life and should accept it.

However, during the early years of the twentieth century society started to recognise that childhood was a stage of development. This resulted in a growing concern that the young were not being treated as they should be. The state began to impinge upon what had previously been viewed as parental responsibilities; school meals, medical examinations of all children, and the Children's Act of 1908 which introduced the idea of child abuse and taking children away from parents and into care.

During the 1920s the idea of 'childhood' became fashionable, a concept much written about in women's magazines. Dr Francis Truby King wrote the *Mothercare Manual* (1923) and Sigmund Freud started publishing his ideas on psychology. But by the 1930s many of Truby King's harsh ideas on the strict upbringing of children were already starting to be revised; a softer approach was developing.

By the 1920s more children were surviving childhood and fewer were being born as a result of the beginnings of 'family planning'. The mean size of households (which included children and servants) had fallen. At the start of the twentieth century there were an average of 4.75 persons per household. In 1911 one sixth of households comprised only two people (compared with one third in 1995). Because they had fewer children and more leisure time parents had more time to spend with their children. Homes were less crowded and leisure activities developed that included the whole family; board games such as 'Monopoly', picnics and days out at the park or in the new motor car.

Clothes manufacturers saw where profits could be made. They started manufacturing clothes specially for designed for children, rather than smaller versions of adult clothes. They were easier to wash and adapted to children's play activities.

Not everything was rosy for children. A misguided government policy started dispatching children to populate empty parts of the Empire; Canada, Australia and South Africa. It was believed that they would have a better life there, away from inner city slums and poverty. Catholic and Anglican churches, Dr Barnardoes homes and the Salvation Army all actively sought children to be sent away, believing that they were giving the children a better life. Children were recruited from orphanages, workhouses and even from the homes of poor families where the parents were struggling to look after them.

Many of these children went across the world never to see their families again, believing that their families were dead or didn't want them. At best they worked as unpaid servants on farms or in houses. Many were treated with cruelty and abused, little better than slaves. During the 1920s questions were raised in parliament regarding the 'children of the Empire'. A special envoy was sent to investigate but she didn't see any need to change a system that was working well for Britain. Families had always been split up in times of hardship and she saw this as an extension of that practice. She concluded that it should continue. The scheme continued until the 1950s.

At the start of the century children were often brought up by people other than their parents. For upper class families the children were looked after by a nanny or by maids. Parents would have the children presented to them for half an hour each day. Once old enough the boys would be sent to boarding school, the girls looked after by a governess.

It was not much better for middle class and working class families. Some middle class boys were sent away to school, but for most children aged 5 to 12 (1901) or to 14 (1920), they would spend their day at the local elementary school, learning their lessons. Then, when they returned home and during holidays they would either have to go out to work to earn a few extra pennies for the family or they would be given tasks to do round the house and then sent outside to play. Children, often as young as two or three, would go out after breakfast and not return until dark. During that time the young children were looked after by older siblings and they would play where they could. Only once it was dark would they return home to be washed, fed and sent to bed.

4.1.   Play, Toys and Pocket Money

Over the years children have always been inventive in their toys, playing with boxes, bits of rope and climbing trees and during the early twentieth century children were no different. With the growing affluence of many families some children were starting to have a childhood, rather than just being sent out to work as soon as possible. They were being recognised as people in their own right.

Many children started to receive regular pocket money during the years between the wars. Middle class families would give three pence (3d) a week, whilst working class families just a ha'penny (½d). However, this was enough for children to buy an ounce of sweets, or a comic. Their money could be supplemented by running errands for family or friends, or when family stopped by for a visit.

4.1.1.   Play

Toys and games were generally owned by the middle class and wealthier members of society. But poorer children in towns and cities were still able to play games and 'hang around' in groups.

During the early years of the twentieth century parents generally left children to find their own entertainment. From an early age they would be encouraged to go and play in the streets (which were clear of traffic at that time) and in woodland or nearby parks. Often they would go with other children, older siblings or on their own. They would climb trees, build dens in woodland or take what they could find to create toys in their imagination.

Children would spend time in the street, the boys shouting and yelling to one another, the girls often minding the baby and watching their antics with amusement and envy. Hopscotch grids were marked out in chalk on the pavements and used day after day in the summer provided the rain didn't erase the marks.

If their parents could afford it a single roller skate could provide hours of fun. Boys would weave and rattle their way down the rough cobbled streets, shouting to one another as they went.

Girls didn't miss out on all the fun. The might have to mind the babies but they would put them all together and then the girls would use an old length of rope for skipping and take it in turns to be 'in'. They would skip for as long as they could before the rough rope wound itself round their legs, leaving red marks to show where it had been. Two other girls would stand, one at each end of the rope turning it round in turn, singing and chanting as the rope burned their hands and slapped the cobbles at each turn.

Boys could become soldiers, with sticks over their shoulders as 'weapons'. They marched up and down the street in groups, shouting and hollering to their friends, taking it in turns to be the officer, screaming commands at their comrades. Their war cries would echo round the street with shouts of anguish as one 'shot' another. Harassed mothers and neighbours would shout at them to be quiet, but it was unlikely that they would take any notice.

On Bank Holidays and Sundays when mother and father were both home they could go on a trip to the park. Mother and children would sit quietly on the grass watching the other children. Father might disappear for a smoke, or to talk with his friends.

On summer days when father was at work and mother busy with the housework the children would take a chunk of bread wrapped in newspaper and head off to the park with their friends. Water could be drunk from the numerous fountains throughout the town. Groups of children would gather, aged thirteen downwards, who would play until late and then return home in time for dinner.

4.1.2. Toys

As the twentieth century got underway there was a growing belief in Britain that children and childhood should be protected and that children needed to be educated and entertained. Part of that entertainment involved the growing number of toys, especially designed to delight children's interest.

In 1902 the first teddy bears were developed simultaneously in the USA and Germany. In the US Morris Michtom developed a stuffed bear after he saw a picture of Theodore Roosevelt with a bear. After sending one of the bears to Mr Roosevelt he obtained permission to use the name "Teddy's Bear". Steiff developed a stuffed bear toy at the same time, first showing it at the Leipzig toy fair in 1903. They rose to instant popularity and were common across Britain in the early twentieth century.

During the 1920s and 1930s, as parents enjoyed a greater standard of living, more toys were developed and sold. Rather than being left to their own devices, children spent more time with their parents, encouraged to play in gardens, back yards or near the house. This is the time when toys that many of us enjoyed as children were first developed.

The Meccano construction toy first appeared in 1907, but was further developed by its creator, Frank Hornby, during the early years of the twentieth century and the range of accessories grew during the 1920s and 30s. A clockwork Hornby train set first appeared in 1921 with the first electric train appearing in 1925, which was further developed in the 1930s and the first OO gauge set appeared in 1938.

Pogo sticks were very popular in the 1920s, as were yo-yos. Monopoly, first developed as an educational device in America during the years of the depression in the early 1930s, first appeared as a board game in Britain in 1933.

Plasticine, Snakes and Ladders, jigsaws, dice, shove ha'penny and darts were popular during the 1920s. Penknives, bows and arrows and kites (whether homemade or shop bought) were also extremely popular. Roller skates and skipping ropes were popular amongst the girls.

Only the very wealthy would have had very many of these toys. There would only have been a few in each house, with siblings expected to share, or toys being passed down from older child to younger. They were more common among middle class children in towns and cities than amongst those in the country or in working class families. There, children were still expected to entertain themselves.

4.1.3. Sweets

The new practice of giving children pocket money was a great incentive for the local shops to stock sweets, especially those that could be bought for a penny or two. Expensive boxes of chocolates, Quality Street and Roses, although available, were out of reach of most children.

Mint Imperials, acid drops, dolly mixtures, sherbet fountains, pear-drops and gob stoppers were all favourites with children with a few pennies in their pocket. Blocks of chocolate could be bought for half a penny (½d) and Turkish Delight for one penny (1d). All were popular and tempted children with a sweet tooth.

4.2. Organisations

Some parents encouraged children to join the Boy Scouts or Girl Guides. The Scout movement started in 1907 when Robert Baden-Powell held a camp for twenty boys at Brownsea Island, Poole, Dorset. By 1910, at their first census, they had over 108,000 members, of which 100,000 were young people. By 1938 there were 400,000 members.

A group of girls asked Baden-Powell to start something for girls and so in 1910 the Girl Guides Association was formed by Agnes Baden-Powell, Robert's sister. In 1914 Rosebuds was formed, renamed Brownies in 1915. During 1914 - 18 Girl Guides acted as messengers for Marconi Wireless Telegraph to transport confidential messages.

There were also the Boys Brigade that had 96,000 members in 1934, the Girls Brigade, Kibbo Kift (founded in 1920) and Woodcraft Folk (founded in 1925).

Several of these organisations became less popular with youngsters during the 1930s as they disapproved of the cinema, smoking, drinking and gambling. They urged members to abstain from these pastimes and encouraged them to take a pledge that they would do so. Those organisations that had religious and military connections (many founded in the Victorian era) soon found their members abandoned them; the lure of commercial leisure activities was too strong.

4.3. Books and Magazines

There were plenty of new books being published during the first years of the twentieth century, such as:

- *Winnie the Pooh* by A A Milne was first published in 1926;
- *The Hobbit* by J R R Tolkein in 1937;
- *The Sword in the Stone* (the first of *The One and Future King* trilogy), by T H White in 1938; and
- *Peter Pan* by J M Barrie in 1911.

To this list, of course, were the list of books that had already been published in the last years of the nineteenth century but remained popular:

- *Treasure Island* and *Kidnapped* by R L Stevenson published in the 1880s;
- *Heidi* by Joanna Spyri, published in two volumes in 1880 and 1881; and
- *The Water Babies; a fairy tale for a Land Baby* by Charles Kingsley published in 1862.

However, books were expensive. Children would have to wait for 1941 and the introduction of paperback by Puffin Books (an imprint of Penguin Books) for books to become affordable.

If books were a little beyond the reach of many youngsters with pocket money to spend then comics and cartoon strips were well within their reach. Some of those that emerged were very popular:

The Daily Express ran a cartoon strip of Rupert the Bear from 1920

The *Magnet* featured Billy Bunter and his bottomless tuck box, the *Gem*, *Champion*, *Rover* and *Skipper* were produced by a growing number of commercial publishers. To these were added *Dandy* and *Beano* from the 1930s.

4.4. Education

By 1901 all children in England and Wales between the ages of five and twelve were expected to attend school and receive a basic education. As a result of this and the restriction on working hours, children were seen as a burden on a family for the first time. Many families would still keep children off school during August to help with farming, or to help as beaters in the fields, in order to contribute towards their upkeep during the rest of the year. The money was essential to a poor family, buying a child's coat or boots for the winter. Because of these regular and numerous absences holidays were extended and schools closed during August.

4.4.1.   Elementary Education

Elementary schools were the basis of the education system in England and Wales during the first decades of the twentieth century. For most children this was their only experience of education.

Children might walk miles each morning and afternoon as a village school would serve the surrounding hamlets and farms. Although their mother would have sent the children out as clean as she could, they would arrive muddy, windswept and wet depending upon the time of year and the weather.

A village school was almost always a single room where all the children would sit either at a desk or on the floor. A fire in the middle of the room gave the only heat during winter months and there was no grill or grate to keep the children from being burned. The room would be freezing cold in the winter, with ice on the inside of the windows first thing in the morning, and baking hot in summer with no air coming through the windows. Children would arrive in wet weather soaked through with no way of drying their clothes during the day.

There was a strict regime. The desks and chairs were lined up row by row in front of the blackboard. Their teacher would stand at the front, trying to keep control of a class of up to sixty children, all at different stages of their education. Her only helper was a pupil teacher, a youngster of about twelve to fourteen years who wanted to stay on at school to learn more advanced subjects. He or she would take the younger children off to a corner of the room to teach them separately. The only deterrent for misbehaving children was the cane, or something, such as a board rubber, being thrown in their direction. The children expected it and the parents made no objection. They had been taught in the same way.

They would learn reading, writing and arithmetic. They were taught by the teacher writing on the blackboard at the front of the class and the children repeated the words, phrases or sums by rote until they were memorised. Tables were repeated: 'once two is two. Two twos are four.' The phrases were shouted, time after time, the children competing to see who could shout loudest, rather than remembering what was being said.

The children would also learn history, geography and popular songs or hymns: 'The Lord is my Shepherd', 'Daisy Daisy' or learning the Lord's Prayer, although they might not understand the words they were saying or singing. Religious education was important in these schools, as it was believed that it taught morals and good behaviour. Sometimes the local vicar would be involved, but often it was left to the teacher to teach the large class as best she could.

During the recession of the 1920s the cost of education to the government came under pressure. Politicians resented the amount of money being spent and local authorities lost much of their funding. Anglican and Catholic schools refused to have more state intervention in their schools, but were unable to pay the amount necessary to retain their independence. The 1918 Education Act had ensured that parents no longer had to pay for elementary schooling, but this left the schools with a hole in their budget.

As part of the government cuts teachers' already low salaries were cut and the class sizes rose. There were minimal facilities in the very basic classrooms. The slates were cleaned with spitting on them and then rubbing them with a cloth, or children could use jotters and pencils. Parents, it was decided, should buy books, slates, jotters, pencils, and anything else needed from the school, but many parents had no money for these extras.

But during all the arguments about funding and who should pay for what, no one questioned exactly what should be taught in schools. It was left entirely to the teachers and head teachers and as a result there was no continuity across the country.

4.4.2. Secondary Education

The 1918 Education Act raised the school leaving age from 12 to 14 (effective from 1920) during which time children should be taught advanced subjects.

During the 1920s three quarters of children aged 11 - 14 in elementary schools received no advanced lessons, just a repetition of those that they had already been taught. Only five percent were given any advanced instruction at all. Almost one quarter of all pupils were determined to leave school before the age of 14 and only seven percent reached grant aided secondary schools.

In 1926 only 9.5% of pupils leaving elementary school went onto secondary school at age 11. There were two types of secondary school. A Secondary Modern (i.e. state run) school and a grammar (private) school.

By 1938 66% of children went onto a Secondary Modern school up to the age of 14. The remainder went on to Grammar Schools to study for the School Certificate (started in 1917 as a qualification for white collar workers and for professional careers). More schools were built in the 1920s whilst the birth rate declined, so it became easier to get a place. However these schools charged fees. From 1907 one quarter of the places were supposed to be awarded free of charge to children who passed the 11 plus exam, who could then attend the grammar school from 11 - 14 to prepare for the School Certificate. In practice though, these places were rarely awarded.

Even when there were no fees, parents often still had difficulty in affording to send the child to the grammar school. It could be the uniform, books, sports equipment and fares they could not afford, or it might be that they simply needed the child to go out to work to bring in a wage. Often parents would only allow one child in the family to attend the Grammar School, often the youngest son, leaving the others to do the best they could at the Secondary Modern School.

Parents rarely thought that it was worth educating the girls in the family as traditionally their role was in the home. Women at this time were still expected to leave work once married, provided the husband was able to support her and often couples would delay their marriage until that time.

Some parents had a mistrust of education. They were born at a time when they expected to be educated according to their status in life. In their view educating a child to a higher level would only lead to a belief that they were better than they were. This was not something they wanted to encourage their children to do. Most people accepted their lot in life with a belief that it was God's will and part of a preordained existence.

During the 1920s and 1930s some schools arranged for girls to spend two afternoons each week doing cooking and some authorities included a further afternoon in a maternity centre or infant welfare clinic. It was believed that this would encourage girls to become good wives and prepare them for keeping a home and motherhood.

4.4.3. Further Education

During the late 1920s and 1930s many teachers at Secondary Modern schools actively discouraged girls from going into service. Some were instead encouraged to go on to two year teacher training colleges (although they may not have wanted to teach), others enrolled in local authority classes in shorthand and typing. Very few went on to study for university degrees. By the 1920s entry to university was available for women. From 1920 they could take an Oxford degree, although Cambridge was slower, only offering women degrees from 1948.

Even for young men it was only a very select few who could go on to further education. The total number of students in higher education (including teacher training) was 52,000 in 1920-1 rising only to 68,000 by 1938-9. This was less than two percent of all 19 year-olds, the lowest figure in any European country. The increase was more because of the construction of new universities offering London University degrees at Exeter, Southampton, Nottingham, Hull, Leicester and Reading, rather than the existing universities relaxing their requirements. Initially the new universities were happy to admit working class students who could remain at home whilst studying, but gradually the places were taken by private school students who could pay higher fees. In 1939 77% of Oxford students came from private schools.

Not many middle- or working-class youngsters could take up places in further education because of the cost. It was estimated that it would cost a student £200 for a student for each year of a degree at Oxford. This was prohibitive for most families. Girls who wanted to study at university were often told their need to study was irrelevant, and even for boys many didn't understand the benefits of having a degree; employers didn't expect, or even want, workers to have one. Of the 554,000 people who took up employment in Britain in 1934 only 13,000 had a degree, less than 2½%.

It was only after the Second World War that the relationship between the economic performance of the country and investment in education was recognised. By this time Britain was a long way behind other European countries.

4.5. Children and Crime

In 1901 children who committed a crime were treated in exactly the same way as adults. They were tried and if convicted they would face the same penalties in the same prisons.

The number of juveniles charged with offences rose from 12,000 in 1910 to 29,000 in 1938. In addition there were many petty crimes that went unrecorded; pilfering sweets, slipping unnoticed into a cinema and scrumping apples from a farmer's field.

In 1908 the Children's Act made provision for a separate court to handle offenders under 16; the Juvenile Court. This gradually developed until the juvenile system (and, for the first time, the appointment of women Justices of the Peace to sit in them) began in 1919. Juvenile courts became a domestic space in which male and female JPs performed gendered roles as parents. Women were expected to understand a child's delinquencies and thus know how best to deal with him or her, whether or not they had ever had children of their own.

Further reform came with the 1933 Children and Young Persons Act, which aimed to get children into education and training with non-custodial sentences for the under 17s and sending 17 - 21 year-olds to borstal or on probation rather than prison (but prison sentences were retained for the most serious crimes). The numbers receiving custodial sentences fell from 53% in 1901 to 45% in 1931 (and to 16% in 1951).

After 1918 magistrates increasingly condemned the use of the birch on youngsters. Traditionally they were sentenced to so many lashes of the birch, usually leaving the skin broken and sore. Magistrates were encouraged to study psychological and medical reports on young offenders which meant they had a better understanding of the young person in front of them. It was claimed that 80% of those birched reoffended. The incidence of birching as a sentence fell from 3,759 in 1918 to 365 in 1926. In certain areas it was eradicated altogether. The Second World War delayed an Act of Parliament ending its use by the courts until 1948.

In spite of recognition by the courts that corporal punishment wasn't working, it continued to be routinely used by both parents and schools until long after the Second World War.

4.6. Courting

Most children left school at 14 and did not marry until their mid-twenties. They enjoyed a time when they were earning money of their own and could take advantage of the growing number of leisure opportunities that were available to them.

Before the First World War young people were still controlled by their parents and by the rules of society. Young women couldn't go out on their own without a chaperon. They still wore clothes that society dictated; heavy, long skirts, tight high necked blouses with corsets under them. Cumbersome clothes that impinged their movement.

However the war opened up many opportunities to young men and women across the country. Men that had been abroad to fight for their country didn't want to return to a life where their parents controlled them. Young women who had stayed at home had done work that they wouldn't have dreamed of doing before the war. They too no longer accepted that their parents should tell them how to behave and to watch their movements every minute of the day. But that said, there were still matters that restricted young couples. Pre-marital sex, particularly in urban areas, was frowned upon and a pregnancy out of wedlock was still a disgrace.

After the war there were an increasing number of places where young people could go whilst courting: Sports and the theatre were places where young people could meet and the back row of the cinema could provide a screen for young lovers.

Weekend promenading around the town until ten o'clock at night was widely accepted by parents as being the acceptable way for young people to meet and attract one another's attention. Young girls would walk around in groups with their friends, waiting to be noticed by a young man who was walking with a group of his friends, trying to catch his eye all the while. Once noticed, they would be asked to the park, or to the cinema. Once there they would get to know one another.

One of the best opportunities to meet was at the dances organised by many churches and other organisations in towns. Here many young people found partners for life. Parents usually regarded this as preferable to meetings on the quiet. The churches hoped that youths would meet people of the same denomination and that nothing untoward would happen. Non-conformist churches often wouldn't arrange dances as they didn't approve of the moral dangers put in a young person's way. However, this often meant that their members would simply go to a dance at another church, often meeting someone from that church and changing denomination.

A meeting at a promenade or a dance could lead to courting, when two young people would see each other more regularly, walking out together. Parents were often reluctant to let a young person marry and leave home, for emotional or financial reasons. But if the duration of the courting was too long then it might promote pre-marital sex, which was frowned upon even in these more enlightened times.

Even those in regular partnerships would not be allowed much time alone together, especially in the evening. Parents, or a younger sibling, would be present when they sat together in the family home, and they were expected to take someone with them when they went out. However trips to the dark back row of the cinema, or to other dances could always relieve the boredom.

These rules were more likely to be strictly adhered to in urban areas, country folk being more relaxed. Country areas would have fewer organised leisure activities and people would be expected to make their own entertainment (carrying on from childhood).

In some areas, sexual experimentation before marriage was almost a tradition. Indeed, as in the past, some families wanted to make sure that a woman was fertile before agreeing to a marriage which was for life. Children were an expected part of marriage, and married couples with no children were pitied.

Illegitimacy rates were 4 - 5% nationally during the first decades of the twentieth century. Although in the country it could be twice that rate, with an unexpected baby being welcomed into the family if necessary without too many questions being asked.

It could take several years for a couple to save for their marriage as setting up home was expensive and it was not unusual for an engagement to last this long. But the marriage, when it arrived, was a celebration for the families involved.

The upper classes tended to rely on the 'coming out' season and presentation at court to find a suitable husband. Hopeful mothers would draw up a list of respectable bachelors, who would be invited to almost every function that they put on. However, young women could still go three or four seasons without finding a suitable match.

5.   Work

Work has traditionally been a central part in the life of British men and women, whether taking place in the home or outside it. Work determined a person's income, social status, friends and leisure activities, and it occupied most of their time. A working class person would have to work 5 - 6 days each week, 50 weeks of the year between the ages of about 15 to 70. It gave a sense of identity, often defining who they were and how they behaved. So when people faced redundancy the feeling of loss and inadequacy was inevitable.

By 1911 agriculture employed fewer than 10% of the population of England and Wales. Many of the old industries were dying and the makeup of the working population was changing. The 1911 census showed that (million people employed in sector):

- 1.2 - mining and quarrying;
- 1.8 - metal manufacture, car industry and engineering;
- 1.0 - textiles and clothing;
- 0.8 - food, drink and tobacco (a rapidly growing industry);
- 1.2 - building industry;
- 1.2 - transport;
- 0.7 - commercial occupations (shops, clerical, lower grades of the professions);
- 0.4 - the professions;
- 2.1 - domestic service.

Of the 71% of men and 29% of women who were in employment 75% were engaged in manual work. The number of skilled and semi-skilled workers was falling and by 1951 the number of them in manual work had fallen to 66%.

5.1.   Changing Patterns of Employment

The most rapidly expanding areas of employment were the middle ranking professions, clerical, administration and technical work, which lead to a growth in salaried workers (as opposed to weekly or piece workers). Between 1911 and 1931 there was an increase of almost 1.4 million salaried workers, of which 650,000 were women. These were generally in the newer industries which were more stable with a higher social status. Social mobility was still possible although more difficult than in Victorian times.

Employment in the coal industry fell from 1.2 million in 1911 to 0.7 million in 1939 and employment in the cotton textiles industry fell from 0.6 million people to 0.4 million.

The modern service industries, which were growing rapidly, took on thousands of workers, but not necessarily in the same areas of the country where people were losing jobs from the old factories, mining and industry. Coal mines and textile mills were in the north of England and the new car industry established itself in Oxfordshire, Coventry and the south. Wholesale and retail distribution on the other hand continued to grow employing 1.7 million in 1920 to 2.4 million in 1938. Employment in entertainment, sport, catering and personal services (such as hairdressing) grew from 2.0 million to 2.7 million between 1920 and 1938.

Those factories that were still profitable were generally the large ones that used semi-skilled and unskilled labour rather than the craftsmen who had previously been needed. Mechanisation and mass production were beginning to undermine the skilled worker, i.e. in the car industry where the coach builder has been replaced with semi-skilled production line workers. They were cheaper to employ and allowed companies to cut costs.

Public sector employers were also taking on large numbers of employees, increasing the size of the civil service, the post office and public sector organisations.

The 'living in' shop assistant that worked for a personal employer (think Selfridges) was being replaced by an employee who worked for a national chain, such as Marks and Spencer and Woolworths. Clerks and secretaries were being employed by big banking groups, communications companies and insurance groups. The skilled office worker was being replaced by standardised procedures and functions, which less skilled people could do at cheaper rates of pay.

5.2.　Hours of Work

Victorian workers worked long, tedious hours. The picture painted by writers such as Charles Dickens in his novels was of the drudgery and hardships on the working class. This was slow to change during the early twentieth century, but there were attempts to reduce the number of hours people were expected to work, especially women and children.

Hours of work were reduced by a 1918 act of parliament which cut the working day from 9 hours (a 54 hour week) including Saturday to 8 hour days (48 hour week). Some industries moved from a two 12 hour shifts per day to three 8 hour shifts. Trade Union agreements played a big part in this move, but they lost much of their bargaining power during the depression when employers were trying to cut their costs and overheads and they had no difficulty in finding workers willing to work whatever the pay and conditions, because there were more applicants than there were jobs.

Although the basic pattern of the week changed it didn't stop those who wanted to take advantage of their workers. Until 1937 it was still legal for women and children to work a 60 hour week in non-textile factories plus 600 hours of overtime each year. Even after 1937 they could be expected to work up to 60 hours each week for half the year, provided the work was seasonal. The Shops Act of 1934 limited young shop assistants to a 48 hour week, but exceptions could again be made for seasonal work.

In 1938 the average number of hours worked by men over 21 was 47.7 hours per week, and 43.5 hours for women, but these averages mask massive variations caused by unemployment, short time working and sickness.

5.3. Trade Union Membership

Trade unions have been legal since Victorian times and during the early twentieth century their membership climbed steadily. During the First World War membership surged and by 1920 there were 8.3 million trade union members, 45% of the potential membership of the workforce.

The growth of union membership before 1914 was encouraged by the unions' success in raising wages and improving conditions for unskilled, semi-skilled and skilled workers alike. They became an influential body when the war made increased demands on industry. They used their power to negotiate wage increases for workers and for political concessions (i.e. rationing and taxation of war profits for employers). This influence continued after the war and resulted in numerous strikes during the early 1920s culminating in the General Strike of 1926.

As workers were not paid during strikes, even a short time off work could tip families into poverty. Trips to the pawnbroker were common, pawning blankets during the summer in the hope they could be redeemed before they would be needed in winter.

The number of working days lost in strikes show how the militancy of unions in the 1920s affected both workers and employers.

Year	Days lost	Year	Days lost
1914	9,878	1930	4,398
1921	85,872	1939	1,356
1926	162,233		

Table 5.1: Number of days of work lost in strike action.

The frequent strikes during 1919 - 1924 caused great hardship and they didn't all achieve the desired end result for the unions or the workers. The General Strike of 1926 was a failure for the trade unions as the government refused to back down.

Their funds were depleted and employees were driven into poverty. The government won and the cuts they had threatened were imposed. After this union membership fell.

5.4.   Taxation

Before the Great War tax wasn't paid on income in the same way as it is today. There were periods in history when tax had been raised, although it was usually only short lived and generally very unpopular.

Rather than an income tax, people paid money to local governments in the form of rates, which were charged on the value of the property they owned or occupied. The amount payable was stated as a number of shillings in the pound of the annual rental value of the property (i.e. 4s in the pound for a house worth £10 per year. 40s or £2 annual payment). This went towards paying for the workhouses, local policing, upkeep of roads and anything else local councillors thought was necessary.

However at the start of the Great War a large amount of money was needed to pay for ammunitions, uniforms, wages and the general war effort. The government imposed an income tax to be collected in addition to local rates. A small amount was collected at first but it increased as the war progressed.

Those people earning less than £160 per year were exempt from direct taxation on their income. However for those earning between above £160 income tax became a harsh reality. By 1919 it was 6s in the pound of income earned, although it was cut during 1924 and 1925 and by 1926 it was 4s in the pound, but it was never abolished, although different governments have imposed differing rates of tax over the years.

In 1929 a married man with two children on £400 per year income paid no income tax. The same man on £500 per year would pay £8 income tax each year.

In additional to the income tax there were also taxes on petrol, motor vehicles and entertainment plus extra duties on tea and beer. These taxes fell to everyone to pay, regardless of their income.

5.5.   Unemployment

Between 1901 and 1910 coal, cotton, shipbuilding, iron and steel experienced boom years. War stimulated demand still further as the factories and mines were pushed to full capacity. A brief boom during 1919- 1920 was the result of people demanding goods they had not been able to get during the war, but it was temporary. In the summer of 1920 demand collapsed. Industries quickly found they had overstretched themselves as foreign demand disappeared. Foreign countries had become self-sufficient during the war and had developed their own manufacturing industries. Once peace returned they continued to manufacture goods at home and imports from Britain were no longer required.

Women were laid off as men returned from the front. Those men who couldn't adapt or move to new industries found themselves out of work. For many this was not short term. In the 1920s unemployment rose to 2 million, 17% of the labour force, something that was unknown before 1914.

By 1929 levels of unemployment were two or three times higher in the old industrial areas than in London and the Midlands, where new industry had already begun to develop. Although all regions were affected by the depression, it was more acutely felt in areas dependent on export sales.

The main crisis in unemployment was in the north. During the 1920s heavy industries were suffering. By 1929 the number of employed coalminers had fallen by 20% from 1914. The number employed in shipbuilding also fell by 20%, as did the iron and steel industry. 25% of shipbuilders were laid off, as were 14% of cotton workers.

In the 1930s those employed in textile, tailoring, boot and shoe, cutlery and potteries were on short time - and short wages. Older men were often the first to be laid off, which left them with little prospect of getting another job.

By 1932 33% of miners, 50% of workers in the iron and steel industry and 66% of shipbuilders were unemployed. For many men finding work meant moving their immediate family away from extended family members and moving to areas where there were jobs in new industries. Men had to re-train for the new trades that were needed. But at the end of the day there was one grim truth - mechanisation of industry cost jobs.

Amongst those in demand were the knife grinders, second hand clothes merchants and pawn brokers. In this time of make do and mend families had to use everything for as long as possible.

Seasonal work caused additional difficulties. Blackpool and Scarborough, like most coastal holiday resorts, had 'slack time' in the winter months when catering staff, stall holders and other service staff were not needed.

Unemployment was regional. Oxford and Coventry, home of the new car plants that were feeding the growing need for cars on British roads, saw almost full employment. Their production lines were staffed by people who were prepared to retrain. But even these jobs were subject to seasonal prosperity. In the early 1920s more people bought cars in the summer months and so staff were on short time during the winter.

Areas in England & Wales	1929	1932	1937
London & SE England	5.6	13.7	6.4
SW England	8.1	17.1	7.8
Midlands	9.3	20.1	7.2
North England	13.7	27.1	13.8
Wales	19.3	36.5	22.3

Table 5.2: Patterns of regional unemployment

Even within the depressed areas there were regional differences. In Wales in 1934 the percentage out of work was 73% in Dowlais, 66% in Merthyr Tidfyl and 73% in Brynmawr. Conditions were less severe in the coastal towns of South Wales and the eastern coalfields suffered more than the anthracite and tinplate districts in the west.

The coal industry accounted for 45.6% of the insured workforce in 1929, but that had fallen to 37.1% in 1935 by the time the worst of the recession was over.

Unemployment caused poverty and impoverished families lost more than just money. Friends fell away when there was no money to travel to see one another. Shopping trips that had once been a pleasure became something of a nightmare; there was not even enough money to buy the essential food needed for the family. Their health suffered, many were depressed (although it was not recognised as such and not understood or tolerated at all well) and women were affected just as much as men. Asthma and bronchitis were prevalent, but there was no money to pay a doctor or even for the transport to his surgery. There was no money for glasses when someone could no longer read, or see well enough to sew and mend the clothes that couldn't be replaced. Abscesses and rotten teeth were left untreated as dentists became a luxury that could no longer be afforded. Times were hard and often extremely painful.

5.6. Middle Class

In the 1920s middle class people were defined as those earning between £250 and £1000 per year. They were largely made up of the professions, forming the upper middle class, down to clerks and white collar workers who were on the lower scale.

Money was central to middle class contentment. With money a man bought or rented his home, sustained his family and put his children through a good education. If he earned enough he could spend the extra on what was important to him; a holiday, stamp collecting or photography (new and rapidly growing hobbies) and on the increasing number of luxury goods and services for the home. There was a good choice for all ages by the 1920s; toys, dolls, train sets, toy soldiers, dolls houses, washing machines, vacuum cleaners, electric or gas cookers, furniture and cars. Anything was possible with a little money to spend.

There were advertisements everywhere that played on what a person might want, encouraging them to spend money on things that, just a few years previously they would never have dreamed of buying. Adverts aimed to persuade women that they could have perpetual youth if they spent money on cosmetics, hair colours and clothes. Advertisements pushed cleaning products by posing the question: 'does your toilet smell?'

It was generally believed that a person's position in the world influenced how they dressed. *Punch* published a cartoon with a basic caricature, showing one man from each class:

- Aristocrats - coronets, robes and a back drop of grouse moors and large country houses;
- Middle class - suits, collars and ties, silk hats for professional men with boaters for the summer.
- Working men - cloth caps, collarless shirts and hands thrust deep in the pockets of dishevelled, baggy trousers.

A cartoon it might have been, but there was definitely an element of truth in what they said.

One academic took this still further (D'Aeth, passim 1910), describing a vertical cross section of society. He declared that there were six basic layers of society determined by income, education, occupation and perceived intelligence.

- Rich - Income over £2,000.
- Upper Middle Class - Senior civil servants, a professional man. Attended public school. Income £600 - £2,000.
- Middle Class - Business and professional people. Income £300 - £600. Attended grammar school. They take an interest in public affairs.
- Lower Middle Class - Shop keepers, clerks, printers, commercial travellers. Income £3 - £5 per week. Attended elementary schools. Have a superficial opinion on all subjects abstracted from popular papers.
- Midway (between middle class and working class) - Skilled artisans, clerks, foremen. They have five roomed homes, comfortable but homely. Income £2 - £3 per week. 'Simple' minds.

- Working Class - Unskilled and casual workers, office boys, shop assistants. Of 'low' intelligence. 18s - 25s per week.

Middle class women were encouraged to keep a distance between themselves and those of a lower class. Distinctions could be seen in church congregations (the rich at the front, the middle class sitting in the centre and the working class at the back). The aristocracy were often seen as frivolous, always spending money on trivial things and obsessed with field sports. But those in the middle class were intense, having to keep working to maintain and increase their wealth. They might not have been as frivolous, but most were just as obsessed with money and what it could do for them. Usually people would only mix with like-minded people of equal class and status.

Professional men defended their territory. They were generally people with a new wealth they had earned rather than inherited. The professions were the elite, not just of the middle class, but they had the intelligence and wisdom that kept the country going. In 1920 E M Forster acknowledged that the middle class had become the 'dominant force in the country'. They were the mainsprings of Britain's greatness (from 'Notes on the English character' Forster Agringer Harvest 19 - 20).

During the war the army had been a great leveller of the hierarchy of society. Because so many junior officers were killed in the early stages of the Great War, many middle class men found themselves promoted to higher ranks. Upper middle class officers would find they were now on a par with the aristocracy. Even working class men found that they had been called upon to save the lives of aristocratic and upper middle class man from their own ineptitude (a common view held by the working class men, and not without basis). But that ended with demobilisation. The officer's pip was not a passport to social advancement and a better job once the war had ended.

Once the war was over, reality for the middle class was as difficult and bleak as it was for working class men. Once they returned from the war they were taking jobs as shop assistants, drivers and porters; whatever was available.

The war destroyed many businesses. The government had dictated what was manufactured, grown, mined and sewn during the war and factories had been commandeered to do whatever was needed. By the end of the war food was rationed and prices were fixed for food, fuel and rent. Taxation, wages and inflation had soared.

By 1919 the advantage that had been with the middle class before the war had disappeared. The system was working against them and, whilst some had profited from war, others received no compensation for their losses.

The trade unions' power now brought middle class employers down. There was a threat from communism which aimed to effectively wipe out any benefit of wealth. Whilst the threat was generally overstated, during the 1920s it felt very real.

After 1918 the middle class were confined by a difficult economy, mass unemployment and instability in Europe. During the market crash of 1929 and the depression that followed many lost much of the wealth they had so far managed to hold onto. This caused some to shift politically to the left as a consequence of the threat from communism, fascism and Nazism and try their hand at politics. Their heyday was over.

5.7. Social Mobility

The key to a better life is education. This, however, was not recognised in the early twentieth century and getting a good education was not easy, even for the middle classes. It was expensive. A University of Bristol engineering course in 1920 cost £26 5s per year, although a reduction to 15 guineas (£15 15s) was given to those whose parents earned less than £350 per annum. Glasgow Technical College charged 12 guineas (£12 12s) per term and teacher training colleges charged £65 - £75 for a two year course.

Living costs had to be added to this. Halls of residence would charge £45 - £65 per year for rent and a student would also need a personal allowance of around £30 per year for food, books and other expenses. A three or four year course would easily cost in excess of £200. Added to which there might be two or three boys in the family who all needed educating, these costs would be out of the reach of many parents. State assistance was minimal. Annual grants of £114,000 were shared between 15 universities.

Getting the capital needed for professional training, education or starting a business was difficult whatever route was taken. Those who didn't possess the capital or who couldn't borrow it from family members would have to stay where they were, whatever their ambitions or motivation.

For the first time parents started to recognise that being able give a child better schooling, i.e. through a Grammar School, would make the difference between that child having to take a manual job and getting skilled work, or even a profession. Many families tried to 'fix' their children's future in this way, only to find resentment and anguish along the way. Not all children had the same determination and drive as their parents.

Among the working classes there were cultural as well as social pressures to stay put. Education, even at Secondary or Grammar Schools, would mean that families would have to go without other things to pay the costs. In spite of these difficulties the middle class continued to expand, although slowly. These problems coincided with the dilution and reduction of middle class influence in society that started in 1914.

Boys often had to commit themselves to an occupation at an early age, through apprenticeships, group loyalties and class solidarity of unions. Women, however, were more likely to be socially mobile. Working women were likely to be in contact with people of higher classes, either through domestic services or their jobs, and were less likely to be members of a union. Domestic service endowed on workers many of the ideas and behavioural manners of the middle classes. Although they might sometimes marry into higher social groups, they were also more likely to pass onto their children a more positive attitude to education and social progression. This could cause friction between the parties to a marriage where the husband was content with his lot, but the wife wanted more.

Teaching was rarely considered, although it was a social advance for the working class. Becoming a shop assistant, although seen as an advance by some, didn't pay enough to bestow middle class status. A more appealing route for many young people was through sport or stage, where the lack of education was not a barrier.

Popular sports were boxing and football, where the money earned would bring them modest wealth, equivalent to that of the lower middle class, on a par with an artisan or shop keeper. The police force was also a means of progression. They recruited from the working class and then separated them from their community, giving them posts away from home. This was a benefit for many trying to escape lowly roots.

During the 1920s people were less likely to follow the main Victorian route out of the working class; setting up in a small business, by buying tea and distributing it, ploughing all profits back into the business. By the 1920s too much capital was needed at the outset and improvements in communications and the development of large chain stores had destroyed much of the local market. Big companies undercut the smaller ones and quickly put them out of business.

The number of self-employed artisans declined during the 1920s as businesses started to use semi-skilled or unskilled workers, laying off craftsmen who might have worked for the same company for many years.

Social mobility gradually became more difficult. Class lines became more rigid in the early twentieth century than they had done in the Victorian period.

Small shops were a very popular way of increasing income. If done well, their owners become valuable to the community, granting credit to wealthy customers and often becoming councillors and local politicians. But the advancement of the

Co-Operative and chain stores, who were able to bulk buy and lower their prices, put many small shops out of business in the 1920s and 1930s.

There were exceptions: Where small shops provided something chain stores couldn't provide. One of these was the fish and chip shop. They were popular to set up because they used a housewife's skills and could be developed to sell pies, cooked meat and tripe. In 1919 a fish and chip shop could be bought for as little as £150. Many returning servicemen used loans offered by the Ministry of Pensions to set themselves up in business. Those unable to find work could use their savings to buy a shop. By the 1930s there were 70,000 employed in this trade and a further 200,000 indirectly involved in selling ingredients and transport. After that prices of the fish and chips were driven down because towns had so many fish and chip shops. It was only the good ones that survived and many had gone out of business by 1939.

A much easier route for an ambitious working class person was by going to work for the expanding commercial intuitions, such as the banks, building societies and insurance companies. In 1911 these industries accounted for 17% of workers, but by 1931 they comprised 23% of the total employment in the country.

6.   Communication

6.1.   Letters

Letters were a commonplace and quick form of communication. They could be short notes asking people to dinner or longer missives updating friends and relatives on a person's life. They were used by businesses to entice new customers or to confirm business that had already taken place. Everyone who could write and who could afford the postage costs used them.

An inland letter weighing less than 2oz cost one and a half pence (1½d) to send in the 1930s. There was an additional charge of ½ d per 2oz for heavier items. Postcards cost 1d to send. There were three deliveries each day in towns and cities, the last at about 5pm. A letter posted in the morning would arrive that afternoon. Letters sent to recipients some distance away took longer, but generally the post was a quick and cheap way to communicate. Even at this time the post was not just for letters. Postmen also delivered magazines, packages of all sizes and mail order goods (seeds, books, clothes etc.). Anything that could be wrapped or put in an envelope could be sent by post.

6.2.   Telephone

The telephone had been invented during the Victorian era and in 1876 Queen Victoria had a line put in from Osborne House on the Isle of Wight to Buckingham Palace. But its uptake was slow. In 1912 the General Post Office took over the small number of private telephone companies that had emerged and from that time the network of connections spread quickly. During the first decade of the twentieth century underground lines were put in between London, Birmingham, Sheffield, Hull and Liverpool and a basic network of trunk lines was in place by 1914.

During the 1920s the telephone became an increasingly important and commonplace part of businesses and homes. In insurance and commerce telephones were part of a new way of trading. Many workers would have one on their desks and would be happy to use them. However, the older professions, including law and banking, were reluctant to embrace change. Letters remained the accepted form of communication and would remain so for the entire period up to 1939.

By the late 1920s many middle class people living in cities had telephones. It was fashionable to 'pass a call', to make a call to one's friends. However, at first there was no direct connection. The person wishing to make a call would pick up the receiver and a voice, speaking very slowly and carefully, would ask 'number please?' Speaking equally carefully the caller would answer with the name of the exchange and the number of the telephone being called. The operator would then connect them with a series of wires and plugs on a board.

Long distance calls were expensive and often not very clear. They needed a series of operators who would connect with each other, until at last the number could be reached. The voice at the other end would sound very indistinct. In 1927 there were 56 lines to the Continent and one radio ink to New York. The cost was extremely high; about £75 for a few minutes conversation.

In 1927 there were about 500,000 telephones in Britain. By 1929 this had risen to over 1.5 million, partly due to the automated exchange, which enabled people to dial direct without the need of an operator. The first such automated exchange was installed in Surrey in 1912, but most could only update after the modernisation of the Holborn exchange in 1927. By 1929, because of the automation, phones started to include dials to enable the user to dial direct. At first this was on the base of a candlestick phone, but in 1929 the Siemens Neophone was introduced. This had a Bakelite base, with a dial and address drawer built in. It had a combined received and mouth piece; the 'one piece handset'. This set the trend for the next 50 years.

Telephones received a mixed reaction. It soon became fashionable to put one's telephone number on a calling card. In some households it was not the 'done thing' to accept a telephone call from someone who had not yet presented their calling card.

The first public call box was installed in Egham, Surrey in 1919. The user lifted the receiver and gave the exchange and number that they wanted. Then a penny was dropped into a slot when the operator asked you to and the call was connected. As telephones spread in popularity coin operated telephones became common in railway stations and post offices.

By 1929 there was still only one telephone to 25 people. They were generally only used by the upper- and middle-classes and the network was limited to the cities and a few major towns. It was slow to reach the more remote areas of the country. Many working class and poor people would not see a telephone, much less have one in their homes, until much later in the century.

6.3.   Telegrams

Even after telephones became a popular way of communicating in towns and cities, country dwellers still had to rely on telegrams because of the limited network of telephone exchanges. Telegrams were relayed in Morse code by cable or wireless telegraphy and could reach an office on the other side of the country in seconds.

Once received at the telegram office, often the local post office, messages were transferred to a standard printed form, either written out by hand or by sticking on the strips of paper produced by the machine that delivered the message. Then the form would be sealed inside a pink envelope and delivered by a uniformed delivery boy who would travel on a red bicycle.

The service cost 6d for the first nine words and 1d for each additional word. This included the name and address of the person it was being sent to so messages tended to be very brief. Often they used words created for brevity; 'exyou' which meant "from you". Such made up words were restricted to five characters in length.

The telegraph was essential to the press. Reporters on the other side of the country could send their report to their office by telegram and it would appear in the next edition of the newspaper.

6.4.   Newspapers

Thanks to improvements in education, the literacy of Britain's population was improving and people were becoming more politically aware of what was going on around them. Newspaper editors and reporters made full use of this and the numbers of newspapers sold and read soared during the first third of the twentieth century.

The number of newspapers purchased daily increased from 4.5 million before 1914 to 10.5 million by 1939. Editors found that good front page news, large headlines and more and improved photographs increased circulation. They added to this a women's page (started by the Daily Mail in 1919) and crosswords which had become a regular feature by 1920. In addition to the daily newspapers, which might have several editions each day, there were the Sunday newspapers which it was estimated were read by 82% of the population.

After the war many towns found that both a morning and evening paper could not be sustained. The Daily News and Daily Chronicle merged in 1930 to form the News Chronicle and the Morning Post was absorbed into the Daily Telegraph in 1937.

The newspaper with the biggest circulation was the Daily Express with 2.2 million copies sold daily in 1937.

6.5.   Magazines

This was a time when people had a growing amount of leisure time and a small amount of surplus cash to spend on themselves and their hobbies. Many magazines sprung up during this time which were added to those already on sale in the High Street and by mail order. Just a few of those available, together with the dates they were founded, are as follows:

- *Amateur Gardening* 1884
- *Amateur Photographer* 1884
- *Apollo* (Book reviews, art and collecting, architecture and more) 1925,
- *British Birds* 1907
- *Country Life Magazines* 1897
- *Golf Monthly* 1911
- *Geographical* 1935
- *Nature* 1869
- *Music Teacher* 1908
- *The Lady* 1885
- *Ladies Companion* (Illustrated monthly magazine on fashions, interesting facts and fiction) 1850
- *Woman* 1937
- *Woman's Weekly* 1911

We tend to think of magazines as being a modern trend with colourful articles and useful tips on a myriad of things. But as you can see, many of the titles that we enjoy today have been around for many years.

6.6.   Books

Nearly 15,000 books were published in 1939 compared with just 8,500 in 1914. There were almost 27 million copies sold, over three times as many as had sold 10 years before.

6.6.1.   Cost

The first decades of the twentieth century books were expensive. A typical hardback book cost 7 - 12s (when a working man's wage to keep a family was £3.10s and a mortgage could be paid for 10s each week), although a cheap edition could be bought for 2s 6d.

Attempts were made to make books cheaper. J M Dent published the Everyman series in 1906 at a price of 1s for each book, and the Daily Herald sold the plays of George Bernard Shaw at 3s 9d plus 6 coupons. Publishers saw this as a threat to their business and they and the majority of authors were against it. They believed that cheaper books were incompatible with literary quality.

Fig 6.1: 'Astronomy' published 1896.

In July 1935 Allen Lane launched Penguin Books, after he had looked in a station shop for something to read on a train, but couldn't find anything worthwhile. His aim was to bring good literary classics to anyone who wanted to read them. He published out of print classics at 6d each, determining that each book should cost no more than a packet of cigarettes.

Fig 6.2: Books published in early twentieth century with cloth covers

W H Smith, who sold newspapers and books at railway stations, publishers and many authors wanted to keep prices high and saw the erosion of the price as a threat to their livelihoods. They certainly had a point. Authors received an average of 20% royalty on each hardback book sold at a cost of 7s 6d. They would only get about 2% of that from Penguin, a huge drop.

However, among the first ten Penguin paperbacks published were *Farewell to Arms* by Ernest Hemmingway, *The Mysterious Affair* by Agatha Christie and *Carnival* by Compton MacKenzie. They proved immediately popular and the catalogue has grown ever since.

6.6.2. Libraries

Because books were relatively expensive most people borrowed them from lending libraries. By the 1930s almost all councils had libraries (having been given the powers to spend public money on books in 1919). Public library loans rose from 85 million in 1924 to 247 million in 1939.

There were also a small number of commercial lending libraries, often run by shop keepers who acquired books from wholesale libraries. They charged borrowers 2 - 3d for each book borrowed. In some areas there were travelling libraries that arrived in lorries, once each month.

Boots lending Libraries offered 2-3,000 novels (45% mystery, 30% romance and 15% western) which catered for many tastes. W H Smiths also had a lending library which charged customers 10s 6d each year to borrow from their collection of novels (50% romance, 25% adventure and 25% crime).

The wealthy would join the exclusive London libraries, such as Day and Munslie, who were happy to cater to their tastes.

A list of popular books is given in Section 14.3 at the end of this book.

7. The Bigger Picture

7.1. Reigning Monarchs and their families

The Victorian era ended on 22nd January 1901 with the death of Queen Victoria at Osborne House on the Isle of Wight. She had resisted many of the changes that were already nudging their way across the country. Changes that would now continue apace under the reign of a new monarch.

7.1.1. Edward VII and Queen Alexandra

Edward VII was 59 years old when he acceded the throne. He had been Prince of Wales for longer than any of his predecessors.

His coronation on 9 August 1902 had been delayed because of negotiations to bring to an end to the Boer War and because he went down with appendicitis just three days before the original date set. So when his coronation finally did happen it was met with relief that he had come through what was then a serious operation as well as being a celebration of his accession.

One of the most memorable legacies of his coronation is Elgar's *Pomp and Circumstance March*, which was written especially for the event. Elgar wrote the music and a master of Eton College wrote the words which have become part of British pageantry.

Edward was very different to his mother, but the British people welcomed the change. He loved beautiful women and fast living. He owned several race horses that had won the Grand National, the Derby and the St Ledger. He enjoyed dinners, usually with at least 12 courses of rich flavours; caviar, snipe, truffles, partridges and oysters. Nothing was too expensive or too rich and he smoked cigars immediately after the meal, flouting tradition.

He was a very public figure, but believed that he should be a man first and a member of the royal family second. He dined at lavish hotels and grand cafes. Twice he was involved as a witness in cases of divorce and cheating at cards, both quite scandalous at the time. Victoria had been a very withdrawn and private person, especially after the death of Prince Albert and had been almost mystical and revered by her people. Edward was very different, and his mother had been concerned about what would happen to the monarchy under his leadership. She would have been horrified. But the people loved him what his mother had seen as his faults were the very qualities that the people loved.

Queen Alexandra was born Princess Alexandra of Denmark, daughter of Prince Christian of Denmark and Louise his wife. Edward and Alexandra met on 24 September 1858 at a meeting engineered by Queen Victoria, who had decided that they should marry. They were friendly from the start and were married at St George Chapel, Windsor Castle on 10th March 1863. Edward was 21 and Alexandra 18.

They had six children. Prince Albert Victor, who died in 1892, Prince George (future George V), Louise, Princess Royal, Princess Victoria, Princess Maud and Prince Alexander who died as an infant.

It was Edward VII who pioneered the idea of royal appearances as we know them today. He opened the Thames Embankment in 1871, the Mersey Tunnel in 1886 and the Tower Bridge in 1894 amongst hundreds of other public appearances. Although he was not allowed a role in running the country by his mother until 1898, he had been frequently seen by the public and was very popular, both as a prince and as king.

Edward VII died on 6th May 1910, just nine years after acceding the throne.

7.1.2. George V and Queen Mary

Edward VII was succeeded by his second son, George V. Being the second son he was brought up with a naval training, his elder brother having been groomed to take the crown. However, on Prince Albert's death in 1892 he was suddenly brought into the spotlight. He proved to be a calm methodical monarch and a strict disciplinarian.

He was a very private man, his hobbies being stamp collecting (of which he evidently had an impressive collection), shooting and yachting. He reigned for 25½ years. Whist Edward VII had showed that the monarchy was still a lively and effective part of the British Constitution, it was George V who had to show what that meant in practice.

His coronation took place on 22 June 1914, just months before the outbreak of the Great War.

His elder brother, as heir to the throne, had been engaged to marry Princess Mary of Teck. After a respectable length of time he was instructed to ask the Princess to marry him, which he did with good grace. They were married on 6th July 1893 at St James's Palace, London. They had five sons and a daughter: Prince Edward (future Edward VIII), Prince Albert (future George VI), Mary, Princess Royal, Prince Henry, Prince George and Prince John who died in 1919.

George V had a reputation as a charmless, distant and irritable man, who shunned the public and insulted the press. He disliked change and was said to hate the radio, aeroplanes, jazz, cocktails and women who wore nail varnish. He was, however, a shy man who found public appearances a trial and showed no interest in 'society'. After a day's shooting he would have a frugal meal, and after an hour with his stamp collection, would retire early to bed. His wife did little to change the public's opinion of her husband. She came from an impoverished family and many believed she and her husband would have been happier living the lives of minor nobility, rather than the heads of the Royal Family.

Although they both worked hard to carry out their duties with effect, they were both cold and distant to their children and to people they met. During their silver jubilee celebrations in 1935 they were said to be stunned to find that they were very popular with the millions who lined the streets to greet them.

Even on the day of his death George V was still attending to matters of state. When signing a document for the Privy Council he refused to allow anyone to guide his hand as he struggled to sign his name. 'Gentlemen,' he is reported to have said. 'I am sorry for keeping you waiting like this. I am unable to concentrate'. He knew what had to be done, however, and he made sure that he did it.

At 9.30pm on January 19th 1936, just a few months after the successful jubilee celebrations, an announcer at the BBC interrupted radio broadcasts to announce that the King's life was drawing to a close. These sombre broadcasts were repeated until, at just after midnight, the director general of the BBC announced that the king had passed away in his sleep.

7.1.3. Edward VIII

In contrast to his father, Edward VIII was a popular, sociable man, keen to party and have a good time. He was blessed with good looks and, at a time when the newspapers were carrying frequent photographs of him, he was recognisable to much of the public long before he acceded the throne on 20th January 1936. His was not a happy reign.

He was the most popular heir to the throne for centuries. He had been made Prince of Wales within months of his father's coronation in 1910 and had been trained from that moment on for the kingship that was to follow.

Unlike his father he was sensitive to the people he met. With his film star good looks he was frequently in trouble with his strict father and cool mother. On a 1924 tour of the USA he was a social success, but his father was furious. His polo playing and dancing until the early hours of the morning, even on a Sunday, had been covered by the American newspapers for days. 'Prince in with the Milkman', 'Here he is, girls - the most eligible bachelor yet uncaught', and 'oh! Who will ask HRH what he wears asleep'.

Even when trying to help the poor in England and in his own principality of Wales he was criticised by the government. His speaking out on the subject in sympathy with the unemployed men he met was seen as criticism of the government's policies. He may have been popular with the public, but he was at loggerheads with the government, who wanted to use his popularity to their own advantage.

Edward first met Ernest and Wallis Simpson at a weekend hunting party. After that Edward and Wallis met at numerous social gatherings and by 1935 the two had fallen in love. She was American, divorced once and on the brink of a second divorce. It had only very recently been accepted that an innocent party to a divorce could be presented at court, so although she had already been presented, the court was unlikely to take a lenient view of the second one.

Technically, once divorced, she would be free to remarry. As king he would be Governor of the Church of England, defender of the faith. That he should want to marry a twice divorced American was unthinkable. At the time of his accession to the throne the public knew nothing of the scandal that was brewing. English newspaper editors had decided amongst themselves not to print gossip or scandal about the couple.

In the summer of 1936, following a holiday on a cruise yacht with friends (Mrs Simpson amongst them) the king decided that he could no longer be king without the woman he loved at his side. The government took the view that he should make a respectable marriage and keep Mrs Simpson as his mistress, as kings had done for centuries. There were three options: that he marry her morganatically (without her becoming queen or their children having any claim to the throne), that he give up the idea of marrying her altogether, or that he abdicate. This king favoured the last, the government favoured the second.

The story broke on 2nd December 1936, just days after a sermon preached by Bishop of Bradford in which he publicly criticised Edward's lack of church going. On December 3rd Wallis Simpson slipped out of the country and went to France to give Edward space to think. The government gave him their ultimatum. Either he abdicate the throne or they would resign. His decision was made. On 10th December 1936 he signed the Instrument of Abdication in favour of his younger brother Prince Albert. On 11th December 1936 he made a radio broadcast to the people of the Empire in which he explained that he couldn't be king without the woman that he loved by his side.

The public was divided. For some it was a wonderful love story and they believed he should have been allowed to marry the woman of his choice, as men and women across the country were how able to do. Others understood the stance of the government and agreed with it. The question had divided the nation and almost brought the British monarchy to its knees.

7.1.4. George VI and Queen Elizabeth

Prince Albert was a quiet man with a stammer. He was shy, had outbursts of temper and had been trained for a life as a naval officer not as a king. On the abdication of his elder brother he was thrust into a life as a monarch without any of the usual training that a prince as heir to the throne would receive.

He had married Elizabeth Bowes-Lyon, daughter of a minor Scottish Lord, in 1923. On the day of their engagement Elizabeth gave an interview to a journalist who had called at her parents' London home without an appointment. She horrified King George V by giving this interview, but he needn't have worried. She was a hit with the press and loved by the public. One million people turned out to see their wedding. It was the first time a commoner had married a royal prince in 300 years.

7.2. Governments

The early part of the twentieth century saw some of the biggest changes to the British system of government and its democracy in history. Those who lived through this period might not have noticed some of those changes but would definitely have known about the others.

7.2.1. Elections

In the general election of 1900 only 3,519,509 people voted. This wasn't because of voter apathy or a tiny population of the UK, but because only men, over the age of 30 who owned or rented property over the value of £10 per year, subject to a 12 month residential qualification, were permitted to vote. This amounted to just 28.5% of the adult population of England and Wales.

At the time people generally had little day to day involvement in politics, other than what they read in the newspapers, unless they were wealthy middle or upper class men. Women had no voice at all. The only way they could get involved was if they were married to a politician and carried out social functions, or if they carried influence with the men in politics, and there were a few.

Working class men and women could only be politically influential if they printed leaflets calling on men and women to write to their local politician or lobby parliament on topics close to their hearts. Some of these leaflets still exist today.

In 1901 politics was dominated by two parties; Conservatives and Liberals. The Labour Party was formed in 1906 from the Labour Representation Committee that had itself been formed in 1900. The government continued to be dominated by Conservatives and Liberals until 1924 when J R MacDonald formed a new minority Labour Government for the first time.

Up until then all major politicians came from wealthy, often titled, families. The Prime Ministers and Chancellors between 1900 and 1939 (see Section 14.5) were earls, viscounts, lords or came from extremely wealthy families. Hardly a representation of the people! However, with members of parliament being paid from 1910 onward working class men were able to enter parliament for the first time.

7.2.2. State Interference

7.2.2.1. Before the Great War

During the nineteenth century the purpose of government was for administration, not for legislation. New statutes were rare and the majority of acts passed were local and private. Acts were needed for divorce or to build a canal. Only rarely were acts passed that affected the whole country. This only changed slowly during the nineteenth century as governments started to act for the benefit of the people; to limit the number of working hours, to ensure better conditions for women and children and for education and public health.

By 1880 the state had assumed control of the worst abuses and ensured rising standards for the majority of its citizens; pollution, adulteration of food, to compel landlords to improve sanitation of dwellings and to give local authorities power (but no obligation) to demolish slums. But local initiative was preferred over central state action, which was seen as excessive and draconian.

During the first part of the twentieth century governments from both parties extended the volume and scope of legislation. They recognised that legislation was needed to help those who were worst off; paupers, the unemployed, sick and elderly and those who were vulnerable. There was no overall plan, but it was the start of a new way of thinking.

The hybrid nature of legislation in the early 1900s was restricted and restrictive. It covered new ground, yet clung to old principles; it understood poverty but believed that any help the state gave should supplement individual initiative, not replace it. It was a safety net and should be unobtrusive. Typified by the local 'Board School' and the corner post office this was the only way most people came into contact with state organisations. Largely those who lived on the right side of the law were left to get on with their lives.

7.2.2.2. During the Great War

This all changed at the outbreak of the Great War. There was a mass movement of men who had volunteered to enlist for the duration of the war, which demonstrated the pride in belonging to a great imperial power. Patriotism and national pride were part of the Edwardian psyche. The books of G A Henty and the *Boys own Paper*, as well as other bestselling accounts of the Boer War promoted an image of war that was both honourable and glorious. There was a pride in fighting for 'King and Country'. But the traditions of individual responsibility, voluntary effort and local government that had shaped Britain were proving to be ineffectual as the effects of war started to bite.

The government made decisions which encroached on normal activities; restrictions on movement of aliens, suspension of dealing on the Stock Exchange, paper notes were introduced for £1 and 10s to replace the movement of gold and the government took on the insurance of war risks on shipping. The Board of Trade took over the running of the railways and there was intervention in the purchase, sale and distribution of first sugar then other food items.

For some any encroachment was intolerable. The trade union movement and the 'No Conscription Fellowship' grew in response to the government's heavy handedness. But most accepted that the government was the most appropriate agency to solve the national crisis. There had been moves in the direction of greater state intervention long before 1914, but it was at the start of the war that most people started to feel the effect.

In 1915 the role of the state was again stepped up. The number of volunteers had fallen and losses on the continent were mounting. There were 350,000 casualties in 1914 - 15, including 75,000 deaths. There was a reduction in the physical fitness requirements of recruits, and many who had initially been turned down were now accepted for service abroad. Mass advertising encouraged men to enlist; 'Kitchener Wants You', 'Women of England! Do your duty. Send your man *Today* to join our glorious Army!' and 'Daddy, what did you do in the Great War?'

The National Registration Act of 1915 required a return for all civilian men and women aged between 15 and 65. This revealed that 1.5 men million were in reserved occupations with 2.25 million already having volunteered. But this left nearly 2 million men still available who had not yet enlisted. All men aged between 18 and 41 were encouraged to register, agreeing to 'attest' (join up) if and when needed. Although not compulsory, moral pressure was added by door to door canvassing. Men who did attest were given an armband to protect them from accusations of cowardice. Married men, it was agreed, wouldn't be called up until all unmarried men had been sent to the front.

But by 1916 it was clear that this still wasn't enough. Out of the 2.18 million single men of military age only 1.15 million had come forward and of the 2.83 million married men, only 1.15 had complied. Additionally, married men couldn't be called up until all single men had been sent to the front. The only answer was conscription, which was introduced in 1916.

Additionally the state started to intervene in the regulation of food and drink. Up until 1915 there had been no restrictions in the opening hours for public houses and many were open all day. But some people started to see that this could be the cause of the high number of people who had a problem with alcohol. Local authorities were given the power to restrict hours as they saw fit and day long opening hours were restricted. But there were still men and women turning up for work hung-over or with the effect of alcohol still evident. So the Central Control Board took over and restricted opening hours to 2.5 hours in the afternoon and 2 - 3 hours in the evening. In addition excise duty on beers and spirits was increased and the gravity of beer reduced. In a short space of time the price of beer increased from 3d a pint to 9d.

Price controls were introduced in October 1917 and by 1919 the price of beer had more than doubled again and consumption had reduced by half. The price of a measure of spirits rose by 500%.

By 1918 there were shortages of imported foods caused by German U-boat blockades and the demand for food for the armed forces. The shortages caused the price of staple foods to rise and many people were unable to even afford the basics. In early 1917 the government introduced controls on meat and by the end of the year, with severe shortages across the country, the government was forced to take over the slaughter and purchase of farm animals and bring all wholesale meat concerns under state control.

By April 1918 meat rationing applied to the whole country. Tea, butter and margarine were also rationed. While bread and potatoes were not rationed they were subject to price controls.

In order to keep morale high, both on the battlefields and at home, the government also controlled information, issuing propaganda where necessary and censoring letters to and from the men and women at the Western and Eastern Fronts. Propaganda enabled the government to manipulate public opinion, both at home and abroad. One early 'plant' of information was that the Kaiser had referred to the British Expeditionary Forces as a 'contemptible little army'. But this was a phrase devised by the British War Office and ascribed to the Kaiser to stiffen resolve of the British troops.

7.2.2.3. After the Great War

After the war ended it took months for men to return home and many years for the effects of the war to ease. For almost all families life was never the same again.

Only in March 1921 was the Ministry of Food finally wound up and state controls on foodstuffs ended. However, many food products remained expensive and difficult to obtain for many years after the war.

It soon became apparent just how much work the government had to do to rebuild the country. The days of the state leaving matters to the people were over. New statutes were put through to allow subsidies for house building, rent restrictions and education. Each year an increasing number of statutes were passed and people found that government intervention now encroached on every part of their lives.

In 1936 driving tests became compulsory for all new drivers. Speed restrictions were imposed on urban roads in 1930, made necessary by the increasing number of accidents that happened every day, but no checks of the roadworthiness of motor cars, lorries and busses were deemed necessary.

7.3. Benefits

In 1901 there were no state benefits to help those who were unemployed, sick or disabled. The poor had to rely on the Poor Law for help, either in the workhouse or as out relief, which could be payment of money or receipt of food or clothing. By 1910 there was a changing attitude to poverty. It was recognised that the state should do more to look after those who, for whatever reason, were unable to look after themselves.

But looking after the poor, sick and elderly was on the low end of the importance scale as far as the government was concerned. National security, national well-being and the glory of the British Empire were considered to be matters of major importance. The desire to rescue and elevate the poor had to come from philanthropists and a few well-meaning politicians. But it was a start.

The provisions of the National Insurance Act of 1911 came into effect at the start of 1913. This scheme provided compulsory insurance for many employed people against the financial consequences of sickness, disablement, unemployment, pensions and childbirth, but not death. Each employee was to contribute 4d per week, the employer added a further 3d and the government paid in 5d. It was intended to be self-funding, with members having to pay into the scheme for a number of weeks before they could receive the benefit.

7.3.1. Sickness

Before the creation of the National Insurance Scheme anyone who was too ill to work received no money either from their employer or from the state. Their only help came from the poor relief which may or may not have helped them.

If the poor relief helped then the Poor Law Guardians made contributions, usually of out relief: money, food, fuel or clothing aimed at keeping the family together and in their own home. The workhouse, as always, would have been there as a last resort if the family became homeless or if the breadwinner was out of work for long periods of time.

From 1913 sick pay was paid to workers who had contributed to the National Insurance Scheme. It paid workers at the rate of 10s per week, the scheme to be administered through approved societies across the country. It was a rate that would have brought about serious poverty, but could, for a short time at least, have kept utter devastation and starvation at bay. But like all benefits under this scheme it was only intended to be a short term benefit, paying out for a few weeks. The length of time the benefit was received depended upon the number of contributions that the worker had made.

7.3.2. Old Age Pension

In 1909 the first old age pensions were paid. Those over 70 and with incomes less than £31 10s per year were paid 5s per week. 490,000 people received this pension, many of them women. It was entirely funded by the state at a total cost of £8 million, a much higher cost than had been expected.

After the 1911 National Insurance Act pensions became contributory and were covered by the scheme. A person needed to have paid into the scheme in order to receive the pension, which paid 10s to those over 65 earning less than £250 per year. It was means tested but the scheme didn't cover civil servants, teachers, insurance officers and salaried people, who were expected to have occupational pensions and so did not need assistance. In 1919 the basic pension was extended to all those over the age of 70 who were in need.

Bearing in mind that Rowntree calculated that a single person needed 20s each week to keep them out of poverty (in 1930), unless an elderly person had another means of income (which, if too high would have meant that they could no longer received the state pension) or rent free accommodation, then 10s per week would have left them almost destitute.

7.3.3. Unemployment Benefit

During the first decade of the twentieth century there was no financial assistance for those who found themselves without employment for whatever reason. Those who had no alternative had to turn to the Poor Law Governors who would decide whether or not the person making the claim was a deserving case. If they were then the help could come in the form of 'outdoor relief', which would be food, fuel, clothing or a sum of money.

In 1913 Britain introduced an unemployment benefit scheme covering 2.5 million people. Workers, employers and the state all made contributions to a central fund. This was always intended to be self-funding and would pay out benefits through the National Insurance Scheme. This included manual workers such as coal minors, iron and steel workers and those employed in the shipyards, although it did not include agricultural labourers, the self-employed or domestic servants. Those not covered would have to resort to the Poor Law for help.

At this time long term and mass unemployment were virtually unknown in England and Wales and in 1920 the scheme was extended to 20 million workers. But this extension coincided with large numbers of people becoming unemployed and the fund quickly ran out of money.

To receive unemployment benefit a man had to have paid six weeks contributions for every week of benefit received. He would be paid a maximum of 15 weeks benefit before being expected to be back in work. Although the government propped up the fund for a short while by paying out money that it had not received in contributions, it soon became economically unviable as the whole country suffered an economic downturn.

An unemployed man would receive 15s for himself, 5s for his wife and 1s for each child in his family. This was about one third of the average weekly pay. Once the 15 weeks benefit ran out, or if the man was employed in one of the occupations not covered by the scheme then he would have to resort to the Poor Law.

450,000 people applied for poor relief in 1920 alone. Although sympathetic (the poor law guardians were elected and wanted to remain so), in order to meet the needs of the current number of unemployed men the poor rate had to be raised to crippling levels, which would have to be met locally.

During the 1920s unemployment rocketed. In 1922 nearly 3 million, almost 25% of the workforce covered by the National Insurance Scheme, were out of work (compare this with 1985 when 3.2 million were unemployed, but this represented only 11% of the workforce). This figure excluded non-insured workers: farm workers, married women and the self-employed.

During the 1920s and 1930s the various governments tinkered with the scheme, trying to find ways of ensuring that only those who were in the greatest need claimed. Married women were dissuaded from claiming, the belief being that their husbands should be the ones to support them. The length of time that the benefit could be claimed was lengthened by Labour governments, only to be shortened again by the National Government. They restricted the 'gaps' between the different benefits and apply different tests to establish whether the benefit could be paid at all.

In 1929 the Poor Law functions were transferred to the newly formed Public Assistance Committee. But they were found to be unduly lenient and so were soon replaced. The problem seemed to be that when the fund administrators, who decided how much each family affected by unemployment should get, could see the hardship suffered it became more than just numbers on a piece of paper. The tiny amounts that the government expected families to live on were unrealistic and caused extreme hardship.

Ignoring these problems the Unemployment Assistance Board was set up in 1934 to manage matters and apply a national, uniform scale of payments. No longer could local generosity and sympathy influence the amount that was paid out. For a family of five the payment was 23s per week in 1922, rising to 29s in 1931 and 36s in 1937. During the financial crisis of 1931 the government imposed a cut in benefits of ten percent right across the board.

Since 1921 efforts had been made to reduce the overall cost to the country and the tax payers. Claimants had to prove that they were 'genuinely seeking work', although the committees were not required to ensure that work was actually available in the area before cutting benefits. Between 1925 and 1928 1.7 million claimants were refused benefits on this basis. Applicants claimed that they were 'treated like dirt'. Any woman who was found to be still breastfeeding her baby was refused as she would not be able to work. Likewise any man found to be sick, disabled or looking after children was also disallowed.

During the financial crisis of 1931 a household means test was introduced. By then the National Insurance Fund was £115 million in deficit and there were 2.6 million unemployed. Change had to happen. Benefits were reduced by approximately 10% and the regulations tightened still further. Married women were excluded from being entitled to unemployment benefit at all. By the end of the year 134,000 married women had their benefit stopped.

At this time the basic rate was 15s 3d for an adult male. But, the whole purpose of the Public Assistance Committee was to save money and during the means testing the assessor would find any reason, however small, to reduce the amount paid and they caused massive resentment amongst the unemployed.

Many skilled and lower middle class workers came under scrutiny for the first time, but the means testing made the unemployed and their families feel as though they were being assessed for the Poor Law and were being labelled as paupers.

The assessment for the 'means test' included 'visitors' visiting the claimant's home and prying into their circumstances. There were occasions when visitors suggested that the claimant could sell certain items of furniture or other belongings and report when they felt that the family had too good a living to need assistance. Relief would be reduced because of savings, income from children or pensioners within the household.

By January 1932 a million unemployed were coming within the scope of the means test. Resources had to be disclosed under threat of legal sanctions should they fail to do so. Large numbers had their claim rejected or the amount reduced. In Lancashire only 16% were awarded the full benefit. A further 33% were disallowed completely.

But £24 million was saved from the unemployment benefits bill by means testing in the first year alone. It didn't seem to matter what humiliation and hardship it caused.

Further changes to the unemployment benefits were made by the Insurance Acts of 1934 and 1935. These acts brought 'black coated' workers within the scope of the National Insurance scheme for the first time. It set up an Unemployment Assistance Board to take over responsibility for the 'transitional benefits' and for all unemployed workers, taking the responsibility away from local authorities. The scheme was nationally administered, with its own scale of payments. The intention was to provide settled and centrally funded benefits for the unemployed.

In 1937 the payment of unemployment benefit of 36s was considered by S B Rowntree, during his investigations into the conditions of the working classes. He found that for a family of five a weekly income of 43s was the minimum required to keep a family above the poverty line. The state benefit fell woefully short of that figure. Hundreds of families were left struggling with poverty and thousands of children left malnourished.

7.3.4. War Pensions

In the 1920s Britain still had 2.5 million war casualties that were sufficiently disabled to be in receipt of a government pension.

Each limb lost was 'costed' on a strict scale. A missing right arm (from the shoulder), 16s per week; 14s if below the shoulder but above the elbow, 11s 6d if below the elbow. The left arm was costed at 1s less for each joint.

But these figures didn't take into account the true effect of seemingly 'minor' injuries; a formerly skilled man would be effectively crippled by the loss of a hand or fingers as he could no longer carry out his profession. Men who were unable to continue with their trade were forced to take menial work to supplement their meagre pension. Every town and city had scores of partially disabled men, drifting in and out of work, often forced into selling newspapers, matches, working as tea 'boys' or bookie's runners.

Those gassed or psychologically scarred fell into different categories, but they would be effectively unable to do any job that involved heavy labour or often any regular work of any kind.

In 1920 People who became blind as a result of the war and who were aged over 50 became entitled to a pension.

7.3.5. Widows and Orphans Benefits

In 1901 there was no state provision for widows or orphans to receive financial help. As one postcard illustrated it, with a picture of a solicitor addressing a widow with three children, "a man may leave his money to whom he likes, but you must maintain your children. That is one of the laws of England". The law had finally recognised that widows had a right to be guardians of their own children after their husband's death (which was not the case before 1886), but would not help them financially. Their only hope was that either private charity or the Church would help them.

Even the 1911 National Insurance Act, which introduced contributory benefits for working men, did not include death benefit or cover for widows and orphans as part of its scheme.

During the war the government introduced a War Widows Pension, paid to women whose husbands had been killed at the front, but they would still not help those whose husbands had died during peacetime.

It was not until 1925 that the state extended benefits to widows whose husbands were not killed in the war. However, it only helped widows of insured men who died after January 1926. For those who died before that date the pension was only paid out if the widow had children under 14 years of age, and then only until they reached that age.

These provisions were relaxed in 1926 when all widows over the age of 55, and younger widows with children under 16 years of age, became entitled to a pension.

7.3.6. Other Benefits

Family allowance was first paid during the Great War to mothers whose husbands were serving in the armed forces. It was stopped after the war and wasn't implemented again until 1946.

The National Insurance Act of 1911 provided for maternity pay to be paid to women whose husbands were covered by the scheme. This didn't include those excluded from the scheme, agricultural workers, domestic servants and the self-employed, who had to claim on the poor law if they had insufficient funds to cover their wives who needed time off when they gave birth.

7.4. Crime and Punishment

A community can only exist by providing rules and insisting on conformity, with penalties imposed on those who don't conform. Those penalties could be imposed through 'custom', such as 'rough music' where neighbours gather outside the offenders house banging pots and pans to show their displeasure, or in more formal ways, such as through the courts by finds and imprisonment.

7.4.1. Crime

The number of crimes known to the police increased during the early twentieth century, although the prison population declined.

Date	Number of Crimes	Prison Population	Crimes Per 1000 population
1900	77,934	17,500	2.49
1905	94,654		
1910	103,132	22,000	2.69
1915	77,972		
1920	100,827	9,900	2.73
1925	113,986		
1930	147,031	11,300	3.99
1935	234,372		

Table 7.1: Number of crimes, prison population and crimes per 1000 of the population.

Those most likely to commit crimes were males aged between 10 and 29 years. Most crimes committed were larcenies (theft) which formed about 75% of the total. Murders, although reported at great length in the newspapers, were uncommon. The crime that increased most was robbery, both simple thefts and breaking and entering homes. Juvenile offences rose from 12,200 during 1910 to 29,400 during 1938, although most of that increase was in the 1930s.

Motoring offences, perhaps predictably, saw the greatest increase. In 1910 there were 55,500 rising to 475,000 in 1938. These were mostly minor offences, although the number of accidents on the road became a big problem during the 1930s.

There was a decline in the amount of drunkenness reaching the courts, 52.6 per 10,000 inhabitants in 1900-9 falling to 12.3 per 10,000 in 1930-7. This was likely to be because of the reduction of opening hours of public houses and an increase in leisure activities available as an alternative to drinking.

At the start of the century poverty related crimes (such as theft of food and poaching) were much more prevalent, decreasing as people generally became more affluent. However, this affluence led to a growing number of thefts, as opportunity increased making larceny easier and more profitable.

England and Wales have always had strict firearms controls and criminal gangs rarely killed; it was just as effective to maim. This meant that razors, cudgels and knives remained the weapons of choice for even the most ruthless criminal. Guns tended to be used by amateur criminals and the desperate, usually to kill themselves or their next of kin. Most criminals who committed theft and non-lethal violence were urban, male and working class. Murder usually occurred within the family or close circle of acquaintances.

Middle class crime was less widespread. It was usually fraud, embezzlement or corruption as opportunities increased with the growing volume of business carried out by local government, businesses and the professions. However, these were a small proportion of the total number of crimes.

There were a growing number of homosexual offences, as this remained a crime. But they only comprised less than two percent of the total number of crimes.

7.4.2. Prisons and Sentencing

At the start of the century there was a continuation in the move towards reformative, rather than punitive, policy in prisons. Prison had proved not to be a deterrent and the use of treadmills and the crank had been condemned in the Gladstone Report of 1895. Greater attention was now being paid to the provision of libraries and communal workshops where new trades and skills could be taught with the aim to provide an alternative means of employment when the convict returned to life outside.

In 1898 the number of crimes punishable by flogging was reduced and a system of classification of prisoners and the provision for remission were introduced. This was still developing at the start of the twentieth century. The probation system started in 1907 and the borstal system and juvenile courts were introduced in 1908.

In 1918 - 1930 there was concern about the growing number of juvenile offenders and the crimes they were committing. Research was carried out and reports written about changes that needed to be made, such as the further development of separate juvenile courts and the use of social and medical reports on offenders. There was also a move to provide education for offenders up to age 17 along with a greater use of non-custodial sentences.

For adult offenders there was a move towards the use of probation and alternatives to custodial sentences, such as fines, which reduced the prison population. Between 1901 and 1931 the proportion of people found guilty of an offence and given custodial sentences fell from 53% in 1901 to 46% in 1931. However, there were large variations between different parts of the country.

Although different sentencing was recommended the courts still had autonomy. The extent to which the new provisions were carried out varied across the country. In 1922 it was estimated that 20% of courts had still not appointed a probation officer, and in 1936 the percentage of persons found guilty of indictable offences and placed on probation varied between 44% and 5% in different courts across the country.

In England and Wales there was a rising crime rate, but the population of the prisons remained relatively stable; mostly because of the increased use of non-custodial sentences. The harshness of the prisons reduced and there was less recourse to punitive task work, humiliation and the use of the 'silent' or 'separate' systems.

Experiments were made in prisons. The first 'open prison' was set up in Wakefield in the 1930s and facilities to improve industrial training inside prison were provided. 'Hard labour' remained on the statute books until 1948 and often prisoners felt there was little reformative effect to the 'useful' tasks they were given in prisons, such as sewing thousands of mail bags. Prison governors retained a considerable degree of discretion and the prison regime remained very grim.

The 'Dartmoor mutiny' in January 1932 was sparked by poor living conditions and the strain created by the imposition of a strict and difficult governor to replace a popular one. Rebellion about the quality of the food and rumours of assaults on prisoners went round the prison. The governor and chaplain were imprisoned in their offices and the prisoners seized the main building and set fire to several others. Warders and police quelled the riot, but not before one prisoner was shot. Although the official report blamed outside agitation, several of the prisoners were tried and convicted for sedition. But changes were made. The governor was removed from his duties and the food and conditions in the prison were improved.

In 1901 7% of persons found guilty of indictable offences, 3,260, were flogged and birched. By the start of the 1940s this form of punishment had almost disappeared. In 1938 only 17 were flogged and 43 juveniles birched.

7.4.3. The Death Sentence

At the start of the twentieth century there was a tendency for a judge and jury to decide that the murderer they had found guilty was 'insane' and 'unfit to plead', which meant that the mandatory death penalty could be avoided. Between 1908 and 1913 32% of murderers were dealt with in this way and committed to a lunatic asylum rather than hanged.

The crime of Emma Thompson, hanged in 1923 alongside her lover, caused outrage amongst the public. Her lover had murdered Emma's husband. She had played no part in the murder other than seeking medical help after the act, but she was found just as guilty as her lover. Females were rarely hung in the early part of the century, just two between 1920 and 1929 and three between 1930 and 1939. Those sentenced to death generally had aroused the moral disapproval of the judge. It appeared that Emma was hanged as much for committing adultery as for the murder. The hangman subsequently resigned his post in protest at the hanging and committed suicide soon afterwards. The move towards the abolition of the death sentence began partly as a result of this case.

The death sentence for desertion and cowardice in the armed forces was abolished in 1930.

7.4.4. Policing

The police force in England and Wales was well established by the start of the twentieth century. The rich were fearful of influence from abroad and the unruly lower classes and by 1918 there was a general belief that the country was about to experience a surge in crime levels. But low levels of crime were tolerated and expected; that of petty theft, burglary, drunken behaviour, domestic violence and prostitution.

There were few detectives at the start of the century. Most serious crimes were solved by paying informants for information. This led to close relationships between those involved in crime and the police force resulting in the involvement of some police officers in the crimes themselves and such occurrences were reported in newspapers once discovered.

In the early 1900s Britain had 190 separate police forces, each with its own staff and complete autonomy. The cost of the police force was £7 million in 1914, rising to £18 million in 1920. But in spite of this high cost they lacked proper resources to effectively deal with crime in their areas but failed to cooperate with each other to work more efficiently.

7.5. The Economy

7.5.1. Boom

During the Edwardian era the performance of the economy had already begun to show signs of weakness, particularly in the heavy industries. In 1914 textiles, iron & steel and shipbuilding accounted for three quarters of all exports and employed one quarter of the total workforce. But Germany and the USA had started to challenge Britain's dominance in the market, developing new industries in chemicals, electrical and skilled engineering. Economic growth slowed by 1920 to just over half what it had been before 1901.

As the country got back on its feet after the war it had to come to terms with a huge loss of manpower. 750,000 men had been killed, thousands more were injured and disabled and could not return to the skilled jobs they had held before the war. Spanish Flu killed a further 150,000 men, women and children, the majority of which were of working age.

War expenditure had totalled £11,325 million, including loans to allies, many of which were never repaid. One third of this was raised by increased taxation and another £500 million was raised by liquidation of overseas assets. But the bulk of it was raised by borrowing. The national debt rose from £650,000 in 1913 to £8,000 million in 1919. Britain emerged from the war as a country heavily in debt.

During the war industries developed only so far as necessary to provide war materials; munitions, uniforms, tanks and food. Usual conditions would have allowed factories and industry to develop new working practices when appropriate, but during the war they had been forced to produce what was needed, rather than what was profitable. During the war exports had been halved and overseas markets lost to those who could supply them; Japan and the USA. Exports never recovered to their pre-war position even once the restrictions ended.

Immediately after the war there was a short economic boom. Speculative development led to rising prices as there was a demand for products that had not been available during the war. In the Lancashire cotton industry 42% of spinning capacity changed hands at seven times pre-war levels in 1919 – 20 and new mills were constructed in expectation of a returning trade. In ship building berths increased from 580 in 1914 to 806 by 1920. Production soared for a while.

7.5.2. And Bust

The collapse began in 1920 with an increase in government borrowing rates, a fall in prices and increasing unemployment. Exports fell still further and a resulting drop in production started to bite. The cotton textile exports in 1922 were less than half of those in 1913. Coal production in 1922 was down 40 million tons from 1913 output and exports were only one third of pre-war levels.

Most industries struggled throughout the 1920s with unemployment rising and exports and production falling. Hopes of a revival were dashed by the Wall Street Crash of 1929. World trade slumped by 35% between 1929 and 1932. This forced Britain off the gold standard and led the government to introduce harsh deflationary measures. Unemployment, a shadow throughout the 1920s, soared still further.

By the mid-1930s new coal fired electricity stations were being built in the North which boosted the demand for coal. But by 1939 61% of coal was cut by machine, which increased production but reduced the need for manpower. New steel plants were built at Corby, Ebbw Vale and Shelton, but these too required less manpower than the older plants they replaced.

7.5.3. New Industry replaces the Old

The mass unemployment and hardship of millions hid the true picture of Britain's productivity in the 1920s and 1930s. By 1924 production had reached levels last seen in 1913, and it was still increasing, and at the end of the 1930s Gross Domestic Product had increased by more than half as much again. In 1935 - 6 the Index of Industrial production was 75% higher than it had been in the period 1910 - 13. In spite of the horrors of unemployment in traditional industries, there was substantial economic growth during the 1930s.

For those living and working in the south, the midlands and those in employment throughout England and Wales there was a better standard of living, more leisure time and more money to spend. Britain was indeed a country of two halves.

In 1920 there were 730,000 homes, one in twenty, using electricity in Britain. By the end of the 1930s there were almost 9 million (one in three) and this figure continued to increase at a rate of 750,000 homes per year. By 1939 this new industry was employing 325,000 people.

Even in the worst years of the slump, between 1927 and 1933, Britain produced more motor vehicles than in any previous year and was a major employer, employing almost 400,000 people by the end of the 1930s in the new factories in Coventry, Birmingham, Luton and Oxford.

The new industries were growing fast, but they were not located in areas where people were losing their jobs. Because of improved rail travel and the development of the new National Grid which supplied electricity nationwide factories didn't have to be located where they could get coal to use as power. They could be located anywhere in the country and the south and midlands of Britain were where most industries chose to be. Unless unemployed people in the north were prepared to, or could afford to, relocate the jobs were not where they were most needed.

7.5.4. Larger businesses

Another major change in industry in the 1920s and 1930s was that with improved transport links businesses didn't have to have all employees and production in one place. The organisation and pattern of business changed from the small family run business to the birth of much larger international corporations spread across several sites and several countries. Mergers and acquisitions were common and from these grew industrial giants, such as ICI, EMI, Unilever and Royal Dutch Shell. These companies traded not just in Britain, but across the world.

Factories tended to be larger, many in the new industries such as Dunlop tyre-making and Nestlé's food production. Ford employed 7,000 people in their Dagenham factory by 1932 and the Hoover factory opened in Penvale on the outskirts of London in 1933.

Mail order schemes became more popular and covered a greater variety of products, made possible by improvements in transport. Motor transport allowed direct delivery to multiple branches of stores. Marks and Spencer's opened 129 stores between 1931 and 1935. Their turnover rose from £2.49 million in 1929 to £23.45 million in 1939, by which time the company had 258 stores.

By 1939 Marks and Spencer's, Lipton's, Sainsbury's and Woolworths had all become household names and there were branches in almost every medium sized town. People could view, touch and buy more food, clothing and household products than they had ever seen before. By 1938 two thirds of all large purchases made were by hire-purchase agreements; furniture, fridges, vacuum cleaners and cookers, all available to people who could not have otherwise have afforded them. Service industries, distribution, transport and administration showed rapid growth, even during the worst years of the recession.

The number of unemployed began to fall after 1935 and, in spite of deflationary measures taken by the government, there was an upturn in trade. Cheap money, protection in the form of government benefits and confidence all contributed to the rapid economic growth in the mid-1930s. Living standards rose for those in work and some parts of the country experienced better prosperity than they had ever had before.

But for those out of work and those regions left scarred by the loss of large industries times were grim. Some hunger marchers, protestors who left their homes in the north of England to march on London hoping to bring their plight to the notice of politicians, recorded their bewilderment. They left their near derelict communities, where three quarters were out of work, and passed through parts of the country experiencing near boom conditions. People they passed were sympathetic, giving them food and sympathy, but they didn't understand the harshness of the conditions these men had left behind.

The economic recovery was not a result of rearmament for what was to come, but from consumer spending. It concentrated on those industries that met people's needs; those that made vacuum cleaners, cars and houses and service industries involving estate agents, insurance brokers and banks.

7.5.5. Wages

A table of average earnings for workers is given in section 14.6. However, these averages conceal many hardships. Some workers earned more, but many were on or below these averages, taking them below the poverty line. In 1938 88% of the population had incomes of less than £250 per year, or £5 per week. Of those 31% had incomes less than £2 10s per week.

	1924	1931	1935
Men and Boys	58.9	57.3	56.6
Women and Girls	24.8	28.0	27.2

Table 7.2: *Average Earnings in Shillings (s) per week.*

The average industrial wage for men and boys was less than £3 per week between 1918 and 1939. However, agricultural labourers were often on less than £2 per week, even in 1939. General labourers, textile workers and some shop workers also fell far below the average wage. But for many the regularity of work, short time working, the amount of over-time on offer and seasonal lay-offs were a continual problem. Alongside this was the ever present concern of unemployment.

The largest proportion of low paid workers were women and juveniles.

8.   The People

8.1.   Birth

At the start of the twentieth century the average number of people in a family was decreasing and by 1920 the two child family was considered the national ideal. Women who married in the 1880s had an average of four or five children. By 1930 the number was down to two. Generally poorer families tended to have the biggest number of children and childbirth was still dangerous.

Fig 8.1: The Green family taken in 1902, shortly after the death of the youngest family member at just a few months old.

In remote areas people still relied upon the 'handy woman' who helped people in childbirth and in death. From 1936 councils were obliged to provide a midwifery service, although the quality of the service provided was sketchy.

Upper and middle class families had their children delivered by a doctor, although again their knowledge and quality varied immensely. Childbirth only accounted for a tiny part of their training and unless they made a point of keeping up to date with current practises they could be more of a problem than a solution. Sylvia Pankhurst discovered that during the early 1900s obstetrics only occupied a brief session at the end of a doctor's course of training. This left many with almost no experience in delivering babies until reaching their practises after qualification.

In the cramped homes of working class people privacy, even in childbirth, was unrealistic. Husbands were sent out in the rain, or they crouched on the front door step, listening to whatever was going on inside. Older children were left to listen, either in the same room or in the next one. A woman struggling with childbirth would try to keep sounds to a minimum, although complete quiet would have been almost impossible. Women still tried to keep everything about childbirth very quiet, not telling children or unmarried women anything about it, the baby simply being presented to the family once born. Some women were still churched, a thanksgiving service for the safe delivery of a new baby, although the tradition was decreasing in popularity even at the start of the century.

First babies, if the family could afford it, were generally delivered in a nursing home, with subsequent ones delivered at home. If the family could afford a nurse once the baby was delivered the new mother didn't set a foot out of bed for five or six weeks. Working class mothers were dependent on what help could be given by friends and family. But the poorest mothers would be up and about almost as soon as the baby was born, cooking, cleaning and looking after the older children and husband. There was no opportunity for recuperation.

8.1.1. Death in Childbirth

Maternal mortality rates (the number of mothers dying in childbirth) was still very high at the start of the twentieth century. By 1923 an average of five mothers died per 1,000 live births. This rose to almost six mothers per 1,000 births in 1933, but had fallen back again to three per 1,000 by 1939.

During the first four decades of the twentieth century it was noticed that there was a marked correlation between medical intervention (by doctors) during the birth and maternal deaths. Doctors used instruments, midwives did not. Additionally, doctors usually came from surgeries, hospitals and even mortuaries to the delivery rooms which could spread diseases. Puerperal (or childbed) fever was spread when the woman was at her most vulnerable. Once infected the mother died within hours.

Doctors in Germany had discovered that if the doctor washed his hands and instruments in chlorinated lime solution after each patient then the mortality rates fell significantly, but this idea was slow to catch on in England and Wales.

8.1.2. Infant Mortality

Infant mortality, although decreasing, was still high at the start of the twentieth century. The highest infant mortality rates were in Cornwall, Cumberland, the upland areas of Wales and Westmorland; all areas where travel was difficult.

In working class families infant mortality was usually a result of tuberculosis, bronchitis, pneumonia, diarrhoea or enteritis. The death rate from bronchitis and pneumonia was nine times higher in babies of unskilled labourers in Durham and Northumberland that children of professional men across England. In the families of professional men, most babies died as a result of congenital malformation and injuries at birth. Marigold (1918 - 21) the daughter of Winston and Clementine Churchill died of a throat infection, something that would have been successfully treated just a generation later.

8.1.3.   Looking after baby

Baby clothes, and items for use by the baby, reflected the family's wealth. The baby of a wealthy family would have a Moses basket, cot, high quality clothes, fine muslin nappies for use next to the skin, cloth nappies, 'mackintosh drawers', rubber pants (to keep the bedding dry from leaking nappies) and fine cotton wear. The baby of a working class family would have to make do with whatever the family already had or were given by family and friends.

Sidney Frankenburg published *Common Sense in the Nursery* in 1922 which recommended feeding at 4 hourly intervals and not at all during the night. He declared that this would allow mother's to lead a 'human' life.

For middle class parents Truby King and his *Mothercraft Manual* of 1924 was the authority. He advised that everything should be done at regular intervals and that the baby should not be 'given in' to and should have as little contact with the mother as possible. Breast feeding at regular intervals was essential, and if the baby was hungry in between then he should be left to cry. The dummy and thumb sucking were strictly forbidden - the baby's arms should be splinted to prevent it if necessary!

By the 1930s Truby King's strict regime was criticised, with mother's being allowed more time with their baby and cuddles being encouraged.

Poorer parents had to improvise. They might use a banana crate for a cot, muslin from food wrappings or cut down shirt tails for nappies. Some even had to use old newspapers for nappies and for the many the baby's bottom stayed bare, with the mother cleaning up when necessary.

8.1.4.   Help during childbirth

It was not until 1902 that the Midwives Act made it illegal to practice as a midwife without being trained. Doctors were unenthusiastic about this as they believed it put midwives in competition with them, even though many doctors were poorly trained in this area. However, untrained midwives continued to practice for home births and everyone turned a blind eye. This was partly because there were so few trained midwives and partly because the poor preferred to use the system that they were comfortable with; calling in the handy woman to help.

By the 1930s more women were receiving professional care at childbirth, mainly because there were fewer births at home. In 1927 just 1 in 27 (just over 4%) births was in hospital. By 1937 this was just over 1 in 3 (35%).

But the 1936 Midwives Act imposed obligations on Local Authorities to train and employ midwives. It was only then that things really started to improve.

8.1.5. 'Family Limitation'

By the beginning of the twentieth century there were several books on the subject of family planning, although the Church still frowned on it as being wrong. Old fashioned beliefs prevailed, that it was a woman's responsibility to populate the Empire and that no woman should use birth control. Up until 1930 the British Medical Association refused to provide information on birth control, even to married women.

Doctors who knew a husband had contracted a sexually transmitted disease from a prostitute would withhold the information from his wife, because 'nothing should interfere with the husband's conjugal rights'.

A 1949 report 'An Enquiry into Family Limitation' found that 84% of those who married between 1910 and 1924 did not 'plan' their families. However, couples tried to 'limit' them rather than 'space' them. Half expected them with a degree of fatalism, aware that there may be 'accidents', rather than 'go in' for children.

8.1.6. Illegitimacy

Illegitimacy rates between 1901 and 1939 was fairly low, an average of 5% of all births, although at the end of the 1930s, when the date of the parents' marriage was recorded on birth certificates, it became apparent that nearly one third of first babies were conceived out of wedlock. Experimentation, especially in country areas, was common. There were a few whose partner absconded, refusing to marry them and the mother was left to bring up the baby with family or have him adopted.

Those who fell pregnant and went on to have the child but didn't marry, had a bleak prospect unless their family was supportive. Often a working class mother would be sent away to relatives in the country to have the baby. The child might be introduced as a child of its grandmother, rather than the family admitting the truth. There is many a story in family histories of a child growing up believing a woman was her sister only to find that she was in fact her mother.

For a working class girl whose family would not support her the only option would be the workhouse. These often had rooms available to admit single girls for the birth of the child. Then the girl would either have to fight to keep the child, or the child would be taken away from her and placed with an adopted family, or left in the workhouse to grow up until he or she was old enough to be placed in an apprenticeship scheme.

In many middle class families the girl would be sent away to a mother and baby home, or relatives in the country, with the child being adopted once it was born. The girl would then return home and the child would never be spoken of again.

8.1.7. Abortion

Abortion, although illegal in England and Wales during this period, was frequently used, and some almost saw it as another form of contraception, even before there was any evidence of the pregnancy. Many girls were confused when attending family planning clinics, where advice would be given on caps, jellies and birth control, but there was a refusal to give any help or advice when it came to abortion. But the nurses were very clear about the distinction and would refuse to give help to illegally 'destroy a life' as it was seen to be at the time.

A government committee, set up to investigate women's views on abortions in the 1930s, found there was a widespread ignorance of the law. Most women questioned believed that it was legal to have an abortion, or to use 'over the counter' solutions, provided it was done before the 'quickening', when they felt the foetus move (usually before the first three months). After that it was only illegal if carried out by a third party. Many women didn't see the foetus inside them as a life.

It was not only the working class, or those in poverty, who believed that a woman was justified in getting rid of an unwanted pregnancy by simple means prior to the mother feeling the child move. Dr Helena Wright, who headed the committee, concluded that middle class women with four or more children did everything they could to terminate subsequent pregnancies believing it to be in the best interests of their family.

For these women it would be decades before terminations (abortions) became legal, and safe, and pregnancy tests could be bought over the counter.

Working class women helped each other. They shared tried and tested methods and the names of sympathetic pharmacists and abortionists. Their self-help prescriptions included 'bumping' down stairs or drinking large amounts of gin whilst in a scalding hot bath. There were pharmacists that advertised pills for 'curing *all* Ladies' ailments', 'getting rid of blockages', or 'National Insurance for women'. However these pills were not cheap selling at 2s 9d to 4s 6d for a box. Sometimes, to try to put the pharmacist in the clear, they would carry a warning that the pills should not be taken whilst pregnant.

A women could also use quinine (with or without tobacco), penny royal, bile beans, Beecham's powders, washing soda, lead from pipes or lead plaster, a potion made by soaking nails and pennies in water or rat poison.

Other women would try remedies that didn't involve ingesting poisons. Slippery elm bark inserted into the vagina using a syringe and soapy water was a commonly used method. The wood swelled when wet, dilating the cervix and causing a miscarriage. Worse still some women would try prodding around with a knitting needle, heated to sterilize it, usually unsuccessfully.

London was the abortion capital. Many abortionists had rooms near the main railway stations, such as Paddington and St Pancras. A back street abortionist in London would charge 2 guineas (£2 2s), whereas a doctor in Harley Street London would charge £50 plus. London accounted for over 35% of all deaths of women caused by abortions.

Abortions were not confined to the major cities in England and Wales. Rural areas accounted for a further 19% of the deaths in women caused by abortions. A midwife in a Welsh mining village working in the 1930s had, over the seven years she was there, witnessed 227 miscarriages amongst the 122 women in the village. Of these only very few, she believed, were accidental.

A survey of 3,000 Birmingham women in 1936 showed that 35% of them had had an abortion.

The government appointed the Birkett Committee to look into illegal abortions in the 1930s. They estimated that around 110,000 abortions were carried out each year of which 66,000 were spontaneous miscarriages (those that occurred naturally) and 44,000 were procured, i.e. illegal. By 1936 the British Medical Association believed that 20% of all abortions were illegal (neither spontaneous miscarriages or carried out to save the mother's life).

8.2. Adoption

Most children were adopted out of necessity, for example when a single mother needed to give a child up, or where a child's parents died or could no longer look after him. The child would be taken in by a family member, friend or someone who wanted a child. But there was no paperwork to follow and sometimes the child never even knew he was adopted.

Before 1926 all adoptions were informal. They might be arranged by a family friend, the doctor or someone of consequence in the neighbourhood for the upper classes. The child would be handed over and there would be no guarantee either that the child would be properly looked after, or that the natural parents would stay out of the child's life. Even after 1926 the working classes still preferred informal adoptions because they had no money to pay the court fees.

Formal adoption was only made possible by the Adoptions Act of 1926, but only people in the upper and middle classes could afford to use the procedure. People who adopted generally preferred girls. They were children to love, not 'foreign blood' that could inherit the family money.

There were three routes to adoption. The Magistrates Court charged a fee of 2s and the natural mother would be called to give evidence that the child could be adopted. In the County Court the fee was £5 and there was a chance that the natural mother would be called to give evidence. It didn't always happen, but it was often enough for it to be a real risk. The High Court charged £60 and the natural mother was never called. This was the preferred route, as the natural parents would never know where the child was taken or who its new parents were, but the adoptive parents didn't always have the necessary money to pay such high fees.

8.3.   Marriage

Before 1929 it was legal for girls to marry at the age of 12 and for boys to marry at 14; but both required parental consent up until the age of majority, 21. However, other than girls who were pregnant, usually at about 15, or for children of the nobility or royalty, it was very unusual for anyone to marry this young.

At the start of the twentieth century most women married at about 25 years of age, and men at 28.

Spinsters were pitied. Without a man's income they were unlikely to ever have a home of their own. In 1921 25% of women aged 30 - 34 were unmarried. In 1931 20% of those in their early 40s were still unmarried. Convention, shortage of money or obligation would keep unmarried children with their parents. Ties to a widowed or sick parent were even stronger.

At the start of the twentieth century marriage was for life. It was believed that partners should be equal(ish) in age, estate (wealth), condition and piety. A suspicion of an inherited disease, insanity or TB would quickly deter potential partners.

By 1931 the average age of marriage was 27 for men and 25 for women. Working class women tended to marry younger. In 1901 34% of women aged between 15 and 39 were married, which increased to 41% by 1931.

Fig 8.2: Marriage of E Sutton to A L Thompson, 1930. Weddings were not the lavish affairs of modern times.

8.3.1. What were they like?

The white wedding dress had been made popular by Queen Victoria when she married Prince Albert in 1840, although they had been known before that. Dresses were expensive and the majority of women, if they could afford it, bought a new dress that they could wear again. In the nineteenth century white had been worn only by the very wealthy, because wearing such an impractical colour demonstrated their wealth. By the start of the twentieth century the colour had become synonymous with weddings.

William Woodruff (1916 - 2008), in his memoirs *The Road to Nab End*, described his sister's wedding. His sister wore a white dress and veil, with lily of the valley flowers. His mother insisted that all the family got new clothes and the groom wore a hired frock coat and striped trousers, seemingly against his will. After the church service the wedding party returned to the family home for a meal of ham, tongue and trifle. The whole party then escorted the newly married couple to the railway station and saw them off on their honeymoon by train, amidst a cloud of confetti and streamers.

Reports and notices in newspapers were popular for all classes.

Weddings were expensive and many working class families got into debt or spent their life savings, just so they could give a good show to family and friends when the daughter of the household got married.

8.3.2. 'Assisted' Marriages

Britain's first marriage bureau opened in April 1939 in Bond Street, London. Heather Jenner and Mary Oliver, both 24 and unmarried, had been presented at court and were said to be happy, sociable women. They saw a niche in arranging marriages for men and women who, for whatever reason, didn't seem to meet the right people when left to their own devices.

In their first week of business they received 250 applications, by post, telephone and in person. The applicants ranged from wealthy widows to country gentlemen and retired officers. The men paid 5 guineas on enrolment and a further 20 guineas on the day of their wedding. Women were charged according to their means, from 10s upwards.

8.3.3. Shortage of Men and the Decline in Popularity of Marriage

Over 750,000 men were killed in the First World War, some married and many unmarried and very young. There were also the ravages of the influenza outbreak in 1918 which killed both men and women, but especially those of marriageable age (see section 13.3.2).

This, coupled with a long-time imbalance between infant mortality of boys and girls which left fewer boys surviving into adulthood, meant that the 1920s started with 1.7 million more women than men in England and Wales according to the 1921 census. Women now had the vote, employment and choice, and the imbalance became more apparent than ever. Women could elect whether or not to marry. Those that did marry could chose to have fewer children. 'Flappers', fashionable young women, had short hair, short skirts, slim hips and no breasts. Many older people thought they were trying to appear as though they were boys and decried it as women moving away from their traditional role. There was a fear that the population of the country would decline to such an extent that it would cause serious problems within a very few years.

During the 1920s and 1930s women's magazines promoted the idea of romantic love and marriage. Marriage was hailed as 'the greatest job of all'. The magazine *My Weekly* debated whether women should propose marriage to the man of their choice - and the answer came back 'yes', they should.

The suggested jobs that a women should take between leaving school and finding and marrying the man of their choice were nurse, library assistant and private secretary. Telephonist was also popular, because 'many a man has fallen in love with a woman's voice'. The magazine painted a dark picture of a woman who remained a spinster by choice in order to follow a career. She would, the magazine insisted, become lonely and neurotic.

Marriage rates dipped during the Great War and the early 1920s, but soon recovered when the average age at marriage fell again. Marriage became more popular as the 1930s progressed.

In 1901 88% of men were married by the age of 49 and this had risen to 93% by the 1930s. The number of women married by the age of 49 was 81% in 1901 rising to 84% by the 1930s.

Even during the economic depression of the 1930s the standard of living for many people had improved, unless they were directly affected by unemployment. This encouraged young people to embark on married life with the expectation of children and a home of their own.

Between the wars young people married earlier and parental control weakened. Wage earning children were often encouraged to move out of the family home so unemployed fathers wouldn't fail the new means test for benefits.

Mass emigration to countries of the Empire that had occurred before the Great War meant that many young women had to travel to far-flung places in order to find a suitable husband. Canada and Australia were popular destinations, where land was cheap and plentiful. India was also a popular destination as industry was booming and there were great opportunities for men with the right skills or a willingness to learn new ones. Two thirds of the men who emigrated in the years 1901 - 1914 were of marriageable age. Women were sent out to find a husband (with an appropriate chaperon of course) who would make a suitable match.

8.3.4. Widowhood

Life expectancy was much shorter in the first part of the twentieth century than it is today. Although marriage was for life, it was generally of a much shorter duration than it is for those who stay together today. Disease and accidents could end a marriage abruptly, which meant that second marriages were common, even though divorce was almost unheard of.

The loss of a wage earner, or the loss of a wife who looked after the children, could pull families apart. Children were sent off to relatives who could afford to keep them, or they would be sent out to work. Many widows or widowers had to look for another spouse as a matter of urgency. Marriage was a practical arrangement, love not looked for quite so much and, although attachments formed, it would not be upmost in the mind of a bereaved partner to the marriage. A man could not go out to work and leave small children alone in the house. A woman who lost her husband usually lost the only wage (or at least the largest wage) coming into the family. Times would be very hard indeed.

Although older children were often left to look after younger ones, compulsory education meant that if older children didn't appear at school then questions would be asked. A permanent solution had to be found - and quickly.

Middle class widows often had to accept a lower status, particularly where their social status arose from that of their husband. Homes and belongings might have to be sold in order to support the family. Many second hand clothes were advertised for sale from a 'bereaved widow who has fallen on reduced circumstances'. Art collections, old furniture and even their houses would be sold to meet their husband's debts and keep the family from starvation.

If the family had no income, then the only place they could get food and shelter was to put themselves at the mercy of the poor law and enter the workhouse. For some it was the only option.

8.3.5. Divorce

In 1901 divorces were exceptional. Only 2 in every 10,000 couples divorced each year. It was expensive and humiliating. The wealthy (the only ones who could afford divorces) believed that infidelity should be managed discreetly. Many unhappily married men and women lead double lives; married in public, but living apart (often with lovers) behind closed doors. Cohabitation was rare, but it could be tolerated if the parties were discrete.

Even working class people, where divorce wasn't possible, could move to another area of the country where they weren't known and set up home as man and wife. Few people would ask questions. They would have children, live and work as part of the community, quietly marrying when their spouse finally died, sometimes many years later.

Marriage was a legal contract and a court order was required to end it. Until 1923 all divorce cases were heard at the High Court in London. By 1918 there were five times as many petitions being heard as there had been before the war, causing too much pressure on an antiquated system.

From 1923 onwards cases were heard at the Assize courts (local courts in major cities across the country) and the system was fully decentralised in 1926, which reduced the cost of obtaining an order. During the early 1920s the annual number of divorces in England and Wales was 2,800, rising to over 4,000 by the late 1920s. 2% of marriages contracted in 1926 had ended in divorce after 20 years, and this rose to 6% of those contracted in 1936.

One of the main causes of the increased divorce rate has been attributed to the increased longevity of the partners in a marriage. Marriages in the late 1800s might have been cut short by death, but in the twentieth century people could be trapped for much longer in an unhappy marriage and so were more likely to look for a way out.

But it was also likely to have been affected by a growing affluence and changing attitudes. People had more money at their disposal. Women were now not just possessions of their husband or father but were people in their own right. They could choose whether to work and divorce could mean a new career and a new way of life, whereas a generation before it would have meant destitution. The social taboos against single women were in decline. Women had a choice.

Once the Matrimonial Causes Act of 1937 became law people could petition for divorce after three years of marriage on the grounds of adultery, desertion, cruelty, habitual drunkenness and insanity. A wife could also petition for divorce if her husband was guilty of rape (of another woman), sodomy or bestiality. After this act became law 90% of petitions were uncontested, although it was suspected that there was a degree of collusion between the husband and wife to reach the result that they wanted.

On an application to the court for divorce the court had the power to impose on the husband a requirement that the husband financially support his existing family before the divorce was agreed. The effect of this depended upon the consequences of the husband and the family.

For the rich the financial consequences were minimal, but they faced possible social ruin which would have been devastating to both parties. But for the poor the situation was far worse. It could be a matter of survival. The husband's income was often so small that he couldn't possibly afford to support two households and this could be enough to prevent the innocent party from suing for divorce in the first place. The law might have changed but the end result was still the same. Only those with enough money could afford a divorce.

Once separation had been granted the parties would have to wait a further six months for the divorce to be finalised. The innocent had to remain innocent during that time. If it was shown that he or she had committed adultery during those six months the divorce would be disallowed.

8.3.5.1. Grounds for Divorce.

Until 1923 evidence of adultery was sufficient grounds for a man to divorce his wife, but the wife would have to prove that adultery plus an aggravating factor, such as cruelty or desertion, had taken place before she could obtain a divorce from her husband.

After 1923 women were given the right to bring a claim for divorce on the grounds of adultery alone. They also had the right to ensure that the husband was denied access to the children if he was shown to be an undesirable influence. For the first time women could gain custody of their children and it was not automatically granted to the husband. In 1937 desertion and insanity were added to the means by which a woman could obtain divorce, at last giving her the same rights as those of her husband.

Only an innocent party was allowed to sue for divorce. If both parties were guilty of adultery and the court found out then the divorce would not be allowed.

A divorced person could not remarry in an Anglican Church.

8.3.5.2. Attitudes to Divorce

Women's Own, the women's magazine, ran articles about how to keep a husband happy once married. 'Looks count after marriage,' ran one article. Another stated 'The happily married man has no more inclination to have affairs with any other woman than his wife desires other men.' 'Dress for your husband. After all, he pays the bills and he is the one to please!' Barbara Hedworth, journalist, claimed that if a man strayed it was the wife's fault for not keeping him happy. Barbara Cartland's strategy was to indulge a husband and pander to his selfishness.

Laura Style, writing in *Woman's Own* in April 1935 stated that 'A bad husband is better than no husband.' She claimed that men needed their freedom. 'The average man gets a fairly raw deal out of marriage in comparison with what he puts into it.' *Women's Own* tried to deter women from divorce. 'Men get their attacks like kiddies get measles... Let him have his fling and he'll come back a thousand times more in love with you than ever.' (*Women's own*, Jan 1934).

The attitudes of 'Agony Aunts' in magazines tended to be bracing. In 1934 'Alex', bored with a life at home and continual domesticity was strongly reproved: 'Just think how many women would gladly give up their so called independence to have a home and a husband of their own... Those who never had a chance because the war took their lovers and their husbands.'

By the late 1930s a woman's aim was 'a handsome husband and a thousand a year'. Most manuals for the single woman originated in America, such as *Live it Alone and*

Like it: A guide for the Extra Woman, by Marjorie Hillis published in 1936. It was full of subjects like 'Etiquette for the Lone Female', and 'A Lady and her Liquor'. For most the lone state was temporary until a man came along. Hillis advocated ways of 'hooking' a man. Take up hobbies such as astrology, palmology and tarot and use them to 'intrigue and waylay men'.

Attitudes to divorce varied depending upon the class that encountered it. The upper class, took a relaxed view to extra-marital affairs, but believed that divorce was shameful and should be avoided. The middle classes considered divorce to be more acceptable and some women believed that it was an opportunity for employment and an independent life. But for the working classes divorce was a disgrace. A mark of failure and very expensive.

8.3.5.3. Number of Divorces

Before 1914 only 25% of petitioners were from the working class. A Royal Commission in 1909 recommended that the working class should be afforded same opportunities as the middle class.

Even after the changes brought about by the 1937 act working class divorces amounted to only a small proportion of the overall number. But the overall number rose by 60% to 7,935 in 1938, and of those nearly 70% had been married ten years or more. The number claiming adultery didn't rise significantly, so it seems to be that the new grounds allowed many to seek a divorce where before they had been unable, or unwilling, to.

The 1937 act changed the grounds and swung it in favour of obtaining divorce from a drunk and cruel husband. By 1934 wives comprised 62% of those seeking the divorce, whereas in 1921 it had only been 41%. The main obstacle was the cost - of both obtaining one and of setting up another household for themselves.

8.3.5.4. Cost of Obtaining a Divorce and Maintenance Payments

Before 1926 Legal Aid, then known as the Poor Persons Procedure, was available for anyone whose annual income was less than £50. This would pay the legal and court costs, but it didn't cover the real cost; the cost of living afterwards.

In the 1930s a divorce cost approximately £50, or £100 if the divorce was contested by one of the parties. This proved to be a deterrent for many people. As well as finding the money for the divorce there were few solicitors who would act as many saw that it would detract from their other cases and they disliked the working classes visiting their offices.

Wives were often deterred by the maintenance arrangements. Before 1920 the wife could be awarded up to £2 per week for her and her children. The 1920 Married

Woman's (Maintenance) Act introduced additional payments of up to 10s per child. In 1925 the Guardianship of Infants Act increased this to £1 maximum.

These maintenance orders could cause immense difficulties for the men expected to pay them, who would often have a second family they needed to support. In 1923 for every 100 orders made, 46 men were imprisoned for default on the payments. By the early 1930s defaulters of maintenance payments comprised 7% of the entire prison population.

8.4.   Old Age

The boundary between an economically active adult and a dependent old person has never been clear cut. Before the Great War there was little help from the state for those who were no longer able to work. For those whose families could not keep them or had no savings to help them would have to go to the workhouse where they would be fed and clothed, although the conditions would be harsh.

By the start of the twentieth century the belief that poverty was part of the natural order created by God was still widespread. The poor accepted their position with resignation, making the best of things as they could.

In 1909 the first old age pensions were paid by the state (see section 7.3.2) but this was far from the panacea it was held out to be and left many old people in desperate poverty.

For manual and unskilled workers it was infirmity that signalled old age. Many went to live with their adult children, but children couldn't always support them, nor look after them properly. A son or daughter would be unwilling or unable to look after the more intimate side of care.

Those in the middle and upper classes could remain independent, or the family could employ nursing help for them. Their lives, though still difficult, were far from uncomfortable.

For those with no other option there was the workhouse, but it was always a last resort. At the end of their lives, even for those whose family had looked after them for a few years, their illness and disability might be more than their families could cope with. For those with a contagious disease the family would not want it transmitted to the healthy adults or children in the house, and for them their only option would be the workhouse.

The workhouse had rooms for elderly and disabled people and they were the only hospitals who would take old people who were unable to pay the cost of nursing care. Those sent to the workhouse went to a place that was demoralising and the quality of patient care extremely low.

8.5. Poverty

Several million people experienced poverty at three times in their lives, a pattern first recognised before the First World War: those under 15 years of age, after marriage when there were young children in the family and in old age. Since the Edwardian era this has largely only affected unskilled workers but for those at or below the poverty line life ranged from utter destitution to a mean and precarious existence when obtaining adequate housing, food and clothing was a constant struggle. But for many their conditions, whilst falling below accepted standards even of the day, had its own structure and values. Those affected could often eke out a makeshift and precarious existence when day to day survival took precedence over everything else. 'Make do' was a way of life.

The majority of people in the early twentieth century were working class and whilst living conditions were harsh they were by no means living in poverty. Many families lived on less than £1 per week (20s) in 1901, but on this they could maintain happy, reasonably healthy lifestyle. But at certain times, when families were large or when there was no work, poverty struck.

Poverty was known to result in poor, overcrowded housing and ill health. In a survey of five towns in the early twentieth century 11% of the inhabitants were recognised as living in poverty, but this figure varied from town to town. A social survey of Liverpool recognised that 16% lived in poverty. The 'New survey of London Life and Labour' in 1934 found that an average of 10% of people were living in poverty although even then there were great differences in different areas; in Poplar and the East End 24% were affected, and in Lewisham just 4.8% were affected.

In a 1937 survey of Bristol Herbert Tout concluded that 19.3% of the population had 'insufficient income' and 10.3% were in 'utter destitution' where any incidental expenditure (such as doctor's fees, mending boots or illness) meant that there was not enough to eat.

The poor were well used to making the best of things. Vegetables could be gathered off the ground at the end of market day, or plucked from allotments when no one was looking. An open fire could be kept going all day on rubbish collected from the street; scraps of paper, potato peelings and wooden boxes. Women and children became expert at finding items that they could burn, just to keep warm or cook what little they could find to eat. But given a certain amount of 'street' knowledge the poor could live remarkably 'comfortable' lives in the strangest of circumstances. But it was precarious, balanced between 'making do' and complete destitution. Dirt damp and vermin were a common part of everyday life.

When doctors attended the houses of the poor they would take a lantern, knowing that their patients often wouldn't have the money for oil or for the electricity meter. Grocers would sell anything, tea, butter or meat, in ounces or a penny's worth.

But for all their cheerfulness and ability to survive the poor had the worst housing conditions, least adequate diet, poorest health and least opportunity to enjoy the new amenities that were springing up in the towns and cities. They had to endure filthy outside toilets that might be shared with up to 35 other people; queuing to use them with no toilet paper, the appalling smell, filth, disease and damp. They were open to the air with a complete lack of privacy. Some women encouraged young children to defecate on newspaper which was then burnt on the fire as a way of avoiding the dreadful outside toilets. Some children knew no different to this. It was a part of their everyday life.

But the poor did manage to frequent pubs and cinemas, fish and chip shops and buy the occasional packets of cigarettes. They would raise a few pennies by holding a horse for a wealthy person, or running errands for anyone who needed them and could pay. Children were especially good at finding money or begging on the street. But it was a mean and squalid life.

8.5.1. Causes of Poverty

The principle causes of poverty were recognised as large families, old age, chronic sickness, losing a wage earner and low pay. It was a known cycle that affected millions of working class people every year.

8.5.1.1. Large Families

S Rowntree in York found that 52.5% of children under 1, 49.7% of children aged 1-5 years and 39.3% of children aged between 6 and 15 lived in poverty. After the age of 15 children could be sent out to work full time to bring in a much needed income for the family. Before they left school many children worked part time, the few pennies they earned bringing relief to the strained family finances. It could be the difference between eating and starving.

H Tout found that in 1930s Bristol one in five children came from a home where the income was below the poverty line. Nine out of ten families with four or more children had an income below a level sufficient to keep the family in adequate housing and health.

8.5.1.2. Old Age

The introduction of the old age pension in 1909 (see section 7.3.2) would seem, on the surface, to have eliminated poverty in old age. But this was far from the case. The amount of pension for one adult was still below the amount needed to keep them out of poverty. Whilst this may have prevented utter destitution which forced elderly people to end their days in the workhouse, it still pushed old people below the poverty line. Unless they could find rent free accommodation or live with adult children they still lived a life of utter misery.

8.5.1.3. Chronic Sickness and Disability

At the start of the twentieth century attitudes to sickness and disability were harsh. Disability, even in old age, was a shameful thing and was often concealed from those outside the family. A sick or disabled person was hidden away until they were no longer around.

With the high number of men left disabled by the Great War attitudes had to change. But they did so slowly. Prolonged illness or permanent disability, whether from the war or by other means, could sink a family below the poverty line. A sick man, no longer able to do heavy manual work, or a skilled tradesman who had lost a hand or suffered paralysis, would have to find menial work which would only pay a small amount. They would be competing for work with young boys and could only expect to be paid the same, a difficult experience for a man used to bringing in a good wage to keep his family.

If a woman had to work to keep her husband then she too would be paid much less than a man who was doing the same job. Life was hard and uncertain, especially if there were also young children in the family.

After 1913 sickness benefit was covered by the National Insurance scheme, but this would only pay a small amount for a limited number of weeks (section 7.3.1). For longer term the family would be dependent on the poor law, either with 'out relief' or by going into the workhouse.

8.5.1.4. Widows

The death of a husband, whatever the social means of the wife, could also herald poverty. Even for the middle classes the loss of a wage earner would mean that the wife no longer had an income and so would have no way of paying rent, school fees or for clothing or food. For many women the only option was to find another husband. Only very few women would be able to find employment to help keep their status, although the simple act of working might well preclude them from their previous status anyway.

After 1925 a widow might qualify for a pension (see section 7.3.5), but the amount was low and would certainly not be enough to keep a home or children. She would either have to eke out a poor existence in a low paid job or exist on the pension itself. Not easy if there was a family to consider.

8.5.1.5. Low Pay

There were large numbers of low paid workers. Their plight was recognised long before the start of the twentieth century, but little was done other than the production of several reports into their problems. Rowntree found that their lives were unlikely to change whilst the wages paid to them were below the minimum needed to maintain a family of any size in reasonable health. Some occupations, even when working full time, didn't pay enough to keep a family in a healthy state.

Those with the lowest pay were the unskilled workers, which included those in the building trades, agricultural labourers, transport workers and municipal and government employees. Seeing an occupation beside our ancestors name on a census return is no guarantee that they lived comfortably. Agricultural labourers' average pay was several shillings below that needed to maintain a healthy family. In coal mining low shift payments and short time working, particularly in South Wales and North East England, left families below the subsistence level.

8.5.2. Help Available

In the poorer areas of towns the pawn shop flourished, not as a resource, but as a part of the weekly cycle of existing from pay day to pay day. Pawning boots or cooking pans meant that the family could raise cash when faced with emergencies, getting them back when better times prevailed. Pawnbrokers would accept anything saleable; clothes, pots and pans, books or a chair. Second hand (or third- or fourth-hand) clothes and furniture could also be bought from them.

There were regimental funds available to help old soldiers, who might need help temporarily or permanently but generally the poor had to find their own way to survive.

8.5.3. Rural Poverty

The labourer's family were frequently saved from starvation by the cottage pig, vegetable garden and a little ingenuity. Meat was a rare luxury and most protein was obtained from cheese.

In Bedfordshire in 1912 the Barrington (Royle, 1997) family consisted of a man, his wife, three sons (10, 8 and 7) and three daughters (13, 5 and 2). The husband worked in a rural lime kiln earning 14s (70p) each week. This was docked in wet weather when he couldn't work. They rented an allotment for 6s 6d (32.5p) per year which provided them about one seventh of their food annually. The family ate mainly bread and home grown vegetables. In a typical week they bought meat which provided dinners, tea and supper for the husband, but this was nowhere near adequate; they received only 49% of the necessary protein in their diet and 42% of energy value needed.

But even in these difficulties meat appeared more widely than it had done 50 years earlier, but it was often only consumed by the man of the family.

8.5.4.   Urban Poverty

This attracted much more attention as it was concentrated in a small area, although in reality it was far less prevalent. The cost of living was higher in towns and food had to be bought rather than grown, but the wages were generally double that of the country. But public health was a much bigger problem and average life expectancy lower.

In London in 1910 A S Jasper (Royle, 1997) described tenement buildings as rat infested, set back some distance from the road, but the front entrances could only be accessed over a filthy, muddy square of waste ground. There was little left of the front doors, behind which rose the rickety stairs to the tiny flats. It was possible for a visitor to see into the squalid rooms from which awful smells emanated, where arguments and screaming children had no privacy.

But if all else failed then the family had no other option but to enter the workhouse, still a horrific and terrifying ordeal for any family up until after the Second World War. Here families were separated and often humiliated. But often the only alternative was starvation.

8.6.   Death

After 1901 the upper class started shunning elaborate mourning and grand funerals. Privacy and simplicity were preferred, although families did not always honour the wishes of the deceased. People often put their wishes into wills and so we can see some of their directions over a hundred years afterwards.

For a poor woman the death of a baby was sometimes a relief. It had been another mouth to feed and when she didn't have the funds, time or energy to look after her existing family, another child could be more than she could bear.

But for many, death was a fact of life. It was one of the constants. People lived, and they died.

The death rate in England and Wales for 1911 - 1915 was 14.3 per 1,000 people. By 1926 it was 12.1 per 1,000 and by 1936 it was 12.0 per 1,000. The average life expectancy in 1910 - 11 was 52 years for men and 55 years for women. By 1938 it had risen to 61 for men and 66 for women. However, these figures hide the fact that there was a huge difference between the classes and between the different regions of England and Wales. But the general trend over the whole country was that people were living longer.

These improvements were largely because of a reduction of infectious diseases: tuberculosis (TB), typhoid and pneumonia. TB was the biggest killer in England and Wales and took 51,000 lives in 1910. By 1940 this had dropped to 27,000.

Infant mortality (due to a variety of reasons) was also a big killer, killing 142 per 1,000 in 1900. But this too was falling, from 110 per 1,000 in 1910, to 82.0 per 1,000 in 1920, 67.0 per 1,000 in 1930 and 61.0 per 1,000 in 1940.

A 1937 'Survey of the Social Structure of England and Wales' attributed lower mortality rates to an improvement in housing, sanitation, hygiene and medical skills. However, in 1933 the death rate amongst poorer people spending 3s per head on food was twice that of more affluent areas spending 6s per head. Contrast the death rates in different areas in 1930 - 2 (per 1,000): Oxford - 80, Cambridge - 73, Rhondda - 134 and Wigan - 138. Even within London the differences were stark: Harrow - 73, Ealing - 78, Stepney - 115 and Finsbury - 128.

Epidemics of diphtheria and whooping cough killed thousands of children per year and a successful treatment was still many years away.

8.6.1. Funerals

In the early twentieth century a death in the family was a part of everyday life. Death was much more 'visible' than it is today.

Most families would call in the 'handy woman', a local woman who helped families with childbirth and the dying.

After someone died he or she would need to be washed, dressed in clothes of the family's choice (or their only clothes if from a poor family) and laid out on the bed. They would then be ready for what was to follow. How elaborate this was, and the choice of coffin, clothes, lace and flowers would depend on how much money the family had to spend. But the family would want to give the deceased as good a send-off as possible.

First the family would get a message to the undertaker. He would come to their home bringing a temporary coffin with him. The body would be placed in the coffin and it would stay in the parlour or main room at home for about a week, which would give the family enough time to make the necessary arrangements.

The family would be invited to the undertaker's house and asked to go upstairs to choose the 'satins, silks and lace edging' for the interior of the coffin from the stock room. Once the coffin was ready the deceased would be transferred into it and would remain there for the rest of the week awaiting the funeral.

Black edged cards would be sent to relatives and friends by post. The telephone was only available in very few places during the first few years of the twentieth century and even if the family had a telephone, it is unlikely that all their relatives and friends would. The receipt of one of these cards was often the first the relative heard of the death.

Since 1837 all deaths have had to be registered at the local registry office in the nearest town and it was the responsibility of the family to do this. If the death was sudden and unexpected then a post mortem would be required, and the death could only be registered once the cause of death had been established. In that case the body would be removed to the rooms of someone who carried this out and then returned to the family once the cause of death had been ascertained, a few days later.

All adult close family members would wear black. The wealthy would have new clothes made, but the working class would wear what they were given or could borrow. Children just wore an armband over their coats, as would distant relatives.

Flowers would be ordered and placed on the coffin at the house and taken to the church for the funeral service with the coffin. Artificial flowers were popular as they could remain on the grave, with a card from the donor, after the funeral and often stayed there for several years.

During that first week the family and close neighbours in the street would close their blinds and curtains to windows that fronted onto the street. On the day of the funeral the whole street would do the same as a mark of respect for the deceased and his family. The church would toll the single funeral bell (if the family could afford to pay the bell ringer) and the whole area would take on a sombre tone.

The coffin would be taken from the house on a funeral byre, a four wheeled handcart that firmly held the coffin as it was taken from the house to the hearse, a glass sided carriage, which was waiting in the street. The hearse would be pulled by black horses with plumes on their heads, a coachman and driver in black top hats and overcoats sitting at the front of the carriage minding the horses. Once the coffin had been placed into the carriage the whole procession would start off. There would usually be other carriages following the hearse, or if the family were poor the family would walk behind the coffin, in order of seniority. The undertaker and several of his men would walk behind the hearse until it reached the end of the street.

If the church was some distance away, or if the family were in carriages, the undertaker and his men would take their seats in the hearse and make their way to the church.

At the church the service was split into two parts. Although cremations had been legalised in 1902 they remained uncommon for the whole period and they were unpopular with older people especially. Burial plots were bought from the church, usually for both husband and wife and for any children that had died young. The poor were buried in graves with no markers as stone headstones were expensive. For paupers there were mass graves, where the exact location of burial is not known.

The service in the church was usually quite short, unless it was a Catholic church when a full mass would be said for the deceased. Once the service had ended everyone moved out to the graveyard and the second part of the service was held around the grave. The coffin was lowered into the grave on long straps and prayers would be said over the top.

This was a sombre and sad service. Men stood bareheaded whatever the weather and women were usually ill prepared for the cold. The minister would spread a handful of earth over the coffin as he recited the words, still used today. 'Ashes to Ashes, Dust to Dust.'

Once the service had been concluded a wake would be held at the family home. A meal would usually be served, such as ham and tongue. Sometimes the will would be discussed, although not everyone made one. In poorer homes a will was quite unusual as the deceased had few possessions to leave.

For the upper and middle classes extravagant funerals became less popular as the century wore on. However, even in the 1930s funerals in working class families in the East End of London were still extravagant affairs and could leave families in debt for many years afterwards.

Corpses of paupers whose family was unable to pay for a burial were given to medical research. In 1934 - 35 of the 261 bodies dissected for medical science only 9 were donated. The rest were the destitute.

8.6.2.   Widows

Widows would embark on a lengthy period of mourning. Black clothes, either newly made, borrowed or donated, were worn for the first three months of deep mourning. After that period grey or mauve half morning was worn, usually for a further nine months.

'Widow's weeds' were veils of black tulle 2 feet square (600mm^2) attached to a woman's hat. This veil could be pulled over the face or left down her back. It was generally only worn during the first period of full mourning.

Many widows and widowers would not remarry until a respectable period had elapsed. However, for some there was the pressing problem of feeding the family, looking after the children or simply surviving. In many instances marriages took place within that 12 month period of mourning, not out of disrespect to the deceased, but out of necessity.

The *Manual of Etiquette* (1908) advised friends of the bereaved to send cards of 'kind enquiry' about a week after the funeral. The family would then send cards thanking them for the enquiry. Only after this reply had been received would it be polite to call on the bereaved widow or mother.

8.6.3. The Cost of a Funeral

In the early twentieth century many working class people had life insurance to cover the cost of a funeral. There was a stigma attached to a wife or husband who couldn't afford a decent send off for someone in their family. If someone had to be buried by the parish then the wage earner in the family would be designated a pauper. Families avoided this if at all possible.

Once a baby was born the parents would pay a penny each week into an insurance policy towards the cost of a funeral should it be necessary. The money would continue to be paid into adulthood. In addition 2d would be paid towards the mother's funeral each week, and 3d towards the father's funeral. It was common for more than one child in a family to die and this was seen as an expedient way of dealing with something that was inevitable – the only question was when it would be needed. In families where money was tight this could cause severe hardship, because money for food was limited, but hundreds of families across the countries paid into these policies.

The cost of funeral in London was approximately two weeks' pay, £2. The cost for a baby or infant would be less, as the coffin was put under a driver's seat rather than using a hearse. This cost could put families into debt for weeks, often putting them into arrears with the rent. The shame of not providing a funeral was worse than the hunger. Neighbours might contribute towards the cost if the family was struggling and there was a collection, but it would be as loan. Working class families couldn't afford to give away money.

The costs for burying a child who died of cholera would include:

- Funeral - £1 12s 0d,

- Death cert - 1s 3d,
- Grave digger - 2s,
- Hearse Attendants - 2s,
- Woman to lay out the child - 2s,
- Insurance Agent - 1s,
- Flowers - 6d,
- Black tie for Father - 1s.

This was more than many families earned and would cause severe hardship for the whole family, in addition to the grief of losing a child.

8.6.4. Mementos of life

Domestic shrines were sometimes set up in the homes of those who died young. Violet Annie Dix (1909 - 19) was the daughter of a Saffron Walden businessman. Her mother kept all her belongings in a trunk in the attic; a posy of flowers she gathered in the garden, letter to Santa Claus, running order of games for a birthday party and darned socks. All were sad mementos showing the impact of her death.

Fig 8.4 War Memorial on the wall of Meifod Parish Church, Powys. Memorials came in all shapes and sizes.

9.   Health and Welfare

9.1.   Illness

The early years of the twentieth century saw great progress in many of the treatments we take for granted today. Insulin was developed in 1922, giving better prospects for diabetic patients. Pneumonia was treated with sulphonamides from 1935 and programs of immunisation from diphtheria and other childhood diseases began in the 1930s. Radium therapy for some types of cancer started to be used extensively from the 1930s onward. Salverson was developed in 1910, providing a safer and more reliable cure for syphilis than the mercury based treatments available up until then.

The Tubercule bacillus had been isolated in 1882, but an effective cure from TB remained elusive until after the Second World War. In the early 1900s the principle treatment for a multitude of ailments remained good food, sunlight, fresh air and rest. In 1911 there were 84 sanatoria with 8,000 beds across England and Wales and by 1930 this had risen to 500 sanatoria and over 25,000 beds.

In the early 1900s TB killed more people in a year than smallpox, scarlet fever, measles, whooping cough and typhus together. Most local authorities maintained isolation hospitals and TB sanatoria until after the Second World War. By 1910 surgery for glands, bones and joints affected by TB accounted for one sixth of all operations.

The 'poverty line' was calibrated after 1914 to be the minimum income that people needed to maintain health. It was recognised that poverty resulted in sickness and ill health. By 1934 nutritional information was available to prove that many of the common ailments and defects were reduced by proper nutrition and food.

In 1922 the Ministry of Health ordered that all milk should be pasteurised before being sold to the public, thus preventing the spread of TB from cattle to humans. Antibiotics, chemotherapeutics and the BCG vaccine were not developed until the 1940s.

Many types of surgery were developed during this era, leading on from experiments carried out during the Great War. There were improvements in brain and lung surgery which continued after the end of the war, experiments with blood transfusions also continued giving better survival rates from serious accidents. Another development was the fixing and of using artificial limbs, unfortunately made necessary by the effects of the war, but it was nevertheless a step forward for medical science.

The New Survey of London Life and Labour, carried out in 1928 – 32, concluded that the improved health of the population was largely due to healthier living conditions, better maternity care, medical inspections of children, the introduction of the Old Age pension and steps to deal with venereal disease. The better diet enjoyed by many was only made possible by higher average disposable incomes and cheaper food prices.

Rehousing people in modern homes, with a sunnier aspect for living rooms and as many bedrooms as possible, a cool larder and fewer projections at the rear of the house which would cut off light and air were recognised advantages that led to better health of the poor who had previously lived in slums. Better sanitation reduced the number of cases of typhoid. Epidemics of infectious diseases were prevented because of lower density developments; there being less overcrowding as more people slept in separate bedrooms.

9.1.1.   Illnesses in Women

The rates of maternal mortality statistics provoked inter-war feminist organizations to push for women's health to be pushed up the agenda. In 1933 the Women's Health Committee Enquiry was established which investigated the health and wellbeing of 1,250 married women and published findings in 1939 as the 'Working-class Wives their Health and Condition'. Many women struggled with their health and most were grateful for any interval of good health between illnesses and pregnancies. The report identified certain ailments: anaemia (558 of the 1,250 women), headaches, constipation with haemorrhoids, rheumatism, various gynaecological problems, tooth decay, varicose veins (exacerbated by childbirth and standing all day), ulcerated legs, phlebitis and white leg.

Only 31% of the women claimed to have good health (suffering only one or two of the ailments listed). 15% had bad health (numerous major and minor ailments) and 31% were in a grave condition and never felt fit and well at all.

The committee held that poor health was partly due to poverty and a reluctance to seek medical help. Few of the women in the study were covered by the National Insurance scheme and so had to pay for any medical advice and treatment. One woman owed her doctor £14 and was paying it off in weekly instalments of 1s. Others put the rest of the family first and stayed away from the doctor to save money, continuing to suffer from whatever ailment troubled them.

In 1937 *Women's Own* advertised Beecham's Pills, Bile Beans, tablets and powders to cure piles, varicose veins, gastric ulcers, constipation, anaemia, neuritis, depression, indigestion, weak nerves, liver and kidney trouble, lumbago, rheumatism and period pains. It gives us a good insight as to what women of the time were troubled with.

9.1.2. Illnesses in Men

Generally throughout this period the general health of men was improving. During the call up for the First World War 66% of men were found to be unfit for duty. During the call up for the Second World War only 33% were found to be unfit for duty. The same system was used for both campaigns.

9.1.3. Illness in Children

Infectious illnesses in children spread through towns, villages and families, often killing several children in one home and many in a street or school. Diseases such as measles, whooping cough, scarlet fever and diphtheria were life threatening to children of any class and tuberculosis was the most common killer in working class children.

It was reported that there was a difference in the height of boys from different classes: poor boys were 2.6 inches shorter than artisans' sons, and 5.8 inches shorter than the sons of professional men. This was largely believed to be due to the differences between their work and food. The food of the poor was condensed milk and margarine, whereas for the rich it was fresh milk, butter, fish, meat, eggs, fruit and vegetables.

Overall though the average height and weight of children was increasing. In the 1900s there was found to be an extra half inch in height per decade in 5 - 7 year olds, and 1 inch per decade for 10 - 14 year olds. There was also an earlier onset of puberty.

By 1939 local education authorities were expected to concern themselves with the health and wellbeing of children. There were medical inspections of children aged 5 - 14 in schools, which included medical, dental and orthopaedic treatment. The authorities became responsible for sanitation in schools and for the control of infectious diseases, systematic physical education and training, provision of school meals, and special open air education for defective children. By 1935 there were 2,300 doctors, 5,300 nurses and 1,650 school clinics. By 1937 school milk was provided for school children either free or at half a penny for one third of a pint to ensure enough calcium was present in their diet for teeth and bones.

9.1.4. Mental Illnesses

Before 1914 the treatment of mental illness had been virtually non-existent. Asylums were widely used, but more as a means of hiding the mentally ill away, rather than for their treatment. The Great War changed that. Men who had had otherwise exemplary service suddenly refused to take orders, or returned from the war changed men. However, even with recognition that mental illnesses were real, there was still only uncertain diagnoses and treatments that were little more than rudimentary.

By 1928 Britain had tens of thousands of men who had a mental illness caused by the Great War and it was at last recognised that their illnesses were every bit as debilitating as physical illnesses and disabilities. It was just that no one knew how to treat them. But more emphasis was at last being put into finding treatments and cures for their problems.

9.2.   Hospitals

During the early part of twentieth century there were three types of hospital.

9.2.1.   Voluntary Hospitals

Voluntary hospitals were charitable organisations funded by donations and fees paid by their patients. Some of the most famous teaching hospitals in London began this way, together with a large number of private foundations in the provinces. By the early 1920s many of these hospitals were struggling financially, with more costly treatments available and more patients to treat.

In 1922 they devised a scheme whereby people earning less than £6 per week could pay 3d a week, which entitled them to treatment in voluntary hospitals at no further cost to themselves. This was a popular scheme, with many firms making bulk payments to cover their employees. By 1939 the majority of people paid for their treatment, either through insurance schemes or by arrangement with the hospital. Only the very poor received free treatment.

These hospitals did remain independent until the start of the NHS and nationalisation in 1946.

9.2.2.   Municipal Hospitals

These were run by local Health Authorities and were funded by local rates. Their treatment was more basic than the voluntary hospitals and they were slow to pick up on new treatments being developed. They generally treated the poor of working age and young children.

There was a great deal of co-operation between the municipal hospitals and the voluntary hospitals, but they did remain separate until nationalisation.

9.2.3.   Poor Law Infirmaries

These too were funded by the local rates. In 1929 when the Poor Law Committees were renamed the Public Assistance Committees these hospitals tried to lose their Workhouse origins, but they found it hard to do so. They treated sick and disabled paupers, who were often elderly but included men and women of working age and children.

In 1928 local authorities were empowered, but not obliged, to take over the poor law infirmaries. Some did so, but a lack of funds meant that many were left to their own devices until nationalisation.

9.2.4. Fear of Change

By 1939 there were 3,000 hospitals of different types in England and Wales. The poor law infirmaries, established in the 19th century, had about 80,000 beds, municipal hospitals had approximately 74,000 beds and the voluntary hospitals had 56,000 beds.

Although they treated many of the same illnesses they were reluctant to be merged, particularly into a state run system. Yet during the 1930s the upward spiral of costs and expenses meant that many wards were closed due to lack of funds. Voluntary hospitals were demanding funds from local authority rates, but at the same time insisting that their independence was crucial and must remain in place. It was not until after the Second World War that change to this antiquated system was made, so that it could cope with the growing population of England and Wales.

Eminent doctors of the early 1900s had become very wealthy on the back of private patients and the fees they paid. They believed that state run hospitals would be a move towards socialism and they had no wish to become salaried medical staff of a state system. But their opposition only delayed what was inevitable and necessary; a state run hospital system.

9.2.5. Fear of Hospitals

Fear of the hospital was widespread, mainly because they still carried the stigma of the workhouse. Many hospitals began life as a workhouse and only changed to a hospital in the 1930s. But history was not easily forgotten by local people. Their fear was not irrational. Hospitals were a place where puerperal (childbed) fever was common, where infectious diseases spread and the standard of care was often very poor. But for those who did need them, they became far more widespread as the twentieth century wore on.

One of the biggest drawbacks of the time was that hospital treatment was not covered by the National Insurance scheme created in 1911 and extended during the 1920s. If a patient needed treatment or became mentally insane, needed a sanatorium or other extensive care, it was only available to those who could afford to pay or to the very poor.

9.3.   Medicines

In the early 1900s medical treatment was carried out by GPs, druggists, chemists, untrained midwives, herbalists, osteopaths and bone setters. The psychoanalyst gained popularity as the century wore on, particularly after the Great War.

Professional treatment became more popular once it could reliably cure illnesses. But for those who didn't trust doctors, or who didn't have the money to consult them except in the most serious of circumstances, there were always other methods to try.

The uninsured, the unemployed who had exhausted their sickness cover and whose name had been removed from lists, dependents of those covered by the National Insurance scheme and the poor and elderly would have to find treatment elsewhere. Almost £30 million was spent on patent medicines bought over the counter in the 1930s. Only if such treatments were ineffective would many seek medical help.

9.3.1.   Self Help

Medical help was costly, both for the consultation with a GP and for the tablets and medicines he might prescribe. Therefore for most people the first course of action was to try self-help remedies.

For coughs and chest problems goose grease was popular or a home concoction of lemon, glycerine and cod liver oil. For pains in the belly prune and fig juice was frequently used. Cuts and abrasions, unless serious, were treated by dabbing on a little iodine.

Only if these remedies failed would many people resort to visiting the chemist or local druggist to try out the cheaper medicines that they had on offer. Chemists and druggists were happy to come up with cures and medicines for a range of symptoms, including dental and eye problems.

If everything else failed, and they could no longer carry out their daily tasks or get to work, then help from the doctor would be sought.

9.3.2.   National Insurance Panel

By 1936 the National Insurance scheme covered 40% of the total population, including 6 million women. It had been introduced to tide people over in times of sickness and provide them with basic medical treatment and medicines from 'panel' doctors. However, this didn't include a dependent wife (except for maternity cover) and children. Those earning over £250 per year had to make private insurance arrangements or contribute to the scheme if they could afford it.

The scheme didn't cover dental and ophthalmic treatment, although some of the larger 'approved societies' who administered the scheme offered them as fringe benefits to attract new customers. For the working class tooth decay and premature tooth loss was a painful part of everyday life.

A GP employing one assistant could have 4,000 panel patients (for which they would receive a capitation fee of 9s 6d for each patient on their books) and a single doctor would be responsible for 2,500 patients. In poor areas where the majority were on the panel each patient would only to receive a cursory examination and basic treatment.

9.3.3.   General Practitioners

Many GPs had few aids to help them in diagnosis: a stethoscope, thermometer, ear syringe and a speculum were all standard. Sterilizing instruments between patients was a dispensable luxury. Doctors had to pay for any laboratory tests themselves, so they tended not to take advantage of any new techniques and treatments being developed. A doctor with a machine to measure blood pressure was considered something special and he would be much talked about in the local area.

Patients were generally happy if they left the surgery with a bottle of medicine, or a box of pills, for which they paid 2-3d. Doctors treating the poor would ask for payment in cash at the time of the visit, but often their fees would depend upon the patient's means and ability to pay. Some people joined a doctors 'club' and pay a small amount each week, or they would go to the outpatients department of the local municipal hospital.

Doctors did not receive a salary at the start of the twentieth century. They relied on fees and the payments received for insurance patients. Those who practiced in poor areas were generally those with more altruistic motives or were less able doctors getting what they could.

In industrial areas a doctors surgery could be in a former shop, with the window painted half way up to allow some privacy. Patients would queue outside, whatever the weather. Some doctors worked from their own homes. Fee paying patients would be given an appointment time, and they would arrive by the front door, shown in by the wife or a maid. Those on the National Insurance panel would arrive by the back door and would have to sit and wait until the doctor had time to see them.

The doctor's surgery would smell of phenol, a sharp distinctive smell. Most GPs performed operations such as hernia repairs, hysterectomies and removing tonsils and appendix for patients, either in their own home or at the surgery. These only happened in cottage hospitals towards the end of the period when the benefits of sterilization became better known.

By the 1930s treatments were progressing. Insulin injections were available in the 1920s, kidney dialysis, radium treatment for cancers, skin grafts and blood transfusions were all available from the 1930s. It was also during this time that treatment for anaemia became a simple iron injection, rather than a sandwich of raw liver as it had been in the past.

9.3.4. Prescription Medicines

Doctors often used placebos, which might be coloured powders, such as red, green or blue aspirin. But as the century wore on doctors had more useful medicines to prescribe.

Aspirin was introduced in 1896 and was widely prescribed. It was available in tablet form after 1914. Quinine for malaria, colchuim for gout, amyl nitrite for angina and opium as pain relief were all effective and used from the early 1900s onward. Sedatives and quick acting painkillers such as morphine and heroin were available from 1898, barbitone from 1903 and phenobarbitone from 1912. But these were addictive, especially for wealthy patients who could afford to keep paying for them.

Immunisation from diphtheria became common during the 1930s and the use of sulphonamides to treat pneumonia and puerperal fever widened from 1935, which meant that these were no longer the killers they had been.

But it was only in 1922 that the General Medical Council altered their regulations to ensure that student doctors were routinely taught about venereal diseases during their training. Until then it was something little talked about and those affected were left to suffer, without the consequences being explained to either husband or wife.

As doctors carried out more successful operations, those operations became more widely used, whether or not they were necessary. Any pain in the stomach was likely to be diagnosed as appendicitis, followed by the removal of that organ. It became fashionable for wealthy people to have their appendix removed before a long sea trip, so as to avoid spoiling the holiday. Children's tonsils were also removed as a fashion, rather than when necessary. This was usually done at the child's home, with ether or chloroform.

9.3.5. Advertisements

Pills, creams and lotions devised to cure a multitude of illnesses and conditions were advertised widely in women's magazines, daily and weekly newspapers and in High Streets. Some were costly, others much cheaper and all classes used them regularly.

It was not until 1939 that advertising 'cures' for cancer available over the counter were banned.

9.3.6.   Tradition and folklore

The tradition of self-prescription and folk remedies remained very strong throughout the early twentieth century. Patent medicines could be brought over the counter at either the druggist or chemist.

In all areas there was folklore, methods of how to cure illnesses and diseases. Some more effective than others. In rural Lincolnshire suffers of whooping cough were advised to go down to the sea when the tide was out, cough into it and the tide would 'take your cough away with it'. In Salford mediums tried to cure varicose veins with herbs and the 'laying on of hands'.

10.   Women

Women's lives arguably changed more during the first half of the twentieth century than at any other time in history. Their place in society, business and politics changed as did how they worked, behaved and dressed.

During the Great War women started to wear makeup, they no longer needed male company when eating out or attending the new cinemas and they could smoke cigarettes in public without fear of reprisals. For the first time women were needed for more than just their domestic role. They were no longer ornamental, fragile people (if in the upper- or middle-classes) or matriarchs who could only work if circumstances made it absolutely necessary. They became people in their own right, and the fight to be treated as men's equal advanced.

By 1939 women were recognised as individuals in England and Wales much more than they had been in 1901. Equality was still a long way off, but things had started to change.

10.1.   Women and the Vote

Before 1918 women, although allowed to enter into some occupations, were not allowed to vote in either local or general elections. They could carry considerable sway through petitioning for their husbands, or persuading their husbands to vote in accordance with their own beliefs, but they were not allowed their own vote at election time.

In 1903 the Women's Social and Political Union (WSPU) was formed by Emmeline Pankhurst and her daughters, Christabel and Sylvia. The campaign was to be fought on a military basis unlike any previous demand for votes for women. In 1907 women became eligible to be councillors, but they were still not allowed to vote in general or local elections. By 1910 those in the WSPU had had enough and wanted to increase pressure on the government. They began a violent campaign for women's suffrage. Their members carried out arson attacks and picture slashing, raising the profile of the movement. Their wrongdoings became widely reported in newspapers and the term 'suffragettes' was used.

They were talked about in social gatherings and meetings across the country, which was exactly what they wanted. Those who had been arrested went on 'hunger strikes' in prison and were force fed, a move which scandalised many in Edwardian Britain. But the government was still only prepared to consider women's suffrage as part of a wider extension of the franchise. The pressure mounted still further in 1913 when Emily Davison (1872-1913) died after stepping in front of the King's horse trying to fix the WSPU colours to him during a race. Over 6,000 women marched at her funeral, carrying banners in the hope that those in power would now listen.

The movement paused at the outbreak of war in 1914. The suffragettes agreed to end their campaign for the duration of the war, provided the government listened to them afterwards.

In 1918, on the cessation of hostilities, the Representation of the People Act came into effect. It granted women over the age of 30, who owned property to the value of £10 per annum, the right to vote in general and local elections. At the same time women became entitled to become Members of Parliament and Lady Astor became the first woman to take her seat in the House of Commons in 1919. But it was only in 1921 that women had the right to vote on exactly the same footing as men, aged 21.

10.2. Women and Property

Before 1925 married women were allowed to own and manage their own property (since 1882) and they were no longer seen as a chattel owned by either their husband or father. They were now independent people. Women had been allowed to vote in parochial councils since 1894, could be made sole guardian of their children if their husband died (since 1886) and were allowed to run their own businesses.

It was unusual for a woman's name to be on the title deeds of a property, or for them to take out a lease in their own name. Wealthy widows or spinsters could maintain their own household, but for the middle- or working-class women it was not so straight forward. They would need a man's wages to be able to take on and keep a home. Rent was expensive and at the start of the twentieth century home ownership was unusual for men, and even more so for women. Equality of pay was still a long way off.

In 1925 women gained the right to be treated as separate individuals in any property transaction, even where their husband was named. This meant that women had a right to be heard and their wishes had to be taken into consideration. By law, they had to consent to property transactions, such as the sale or mortgage of a home, where they were named on the title deeds.

10.3. Fashions and Hair

Not only did women's political and legal status change during the first half of the twentieth century, but so too did what they wore and how they saw themselves. It started almost as soon as the new century dawned, but accelerated during the Great War. Then, as now, clothes were a badge of social origin and income.

10.3.1. Edwardian Fashions

Almost as soon as the old queen had died fashions started to change. King Edward VII was a very different monarch; a fun loving, socially minded man who loved nothing more than extravagant living and sport. Women quickly found that the old heavy fashions of Victorian England were best left behind and Queen Alexandra led the way.

The long skirts of the Victorian era soon edged above the ankle. The materials were still heavy and thick, wools, tweeds and cottons, but the cut emphasised the hour-glass, feminine look, with high necked blouses and flouncy, trailing skirts for the wealthy. Whalebone corsets and starched cotton petticoats smoothed the lines of less than perfect figures.

Middle class women who wanted to copy the upper class fashions bought high quality clothes from second hand clothes merchants. In this way the less well-off could copy the fashions and dress better than they could otherwise afford. There were always people willing to sell, either widows who found themselves on reduced circumstances, or the wealthy selling off last month's clothes to make room for the new.

In tenements the shawl that women clutched round their body was a symbol of respectability. It functioned as a coat and jacket for those who could afford neither, keeping away cold and damp conditions.

For the poor though it was the same as it had always been. They wore what they had to hand, either hand-me-downs from better off relatives or bought clothes second hand from market stalls. They might have only one dress to their name, with a threadbare shawl slung round their shoulders and over their head in the coldest weather to keep out the rain and ice. Their underclothes would be washed overnight or at the end of the week and would have to be mended and pressed into use once again.

Make up was still frowned upon and when used it had to be very discrete. It was only used in any quantity by those on the stage and ladies of ill repute. Lip colouring was unusual, but respectable ladies could add a little colour to their cheeks and kohl shadows to the eyes. Mascara was thickened with coconut oil on eyelashes and lightly coloured, highly polished fingernails became popular.

10.3.2.   Effect of the Great War

The war had an unexpected effect on women's clothing. Because of a shortage of material, much of it having to go to make uniforms for the men at the front, skirts became shorter and hemlines rose. For women it became patriotic to wear shorter skirts as they had foregone fashions for the benefit of the war effort. But as hemlines rose women found it offered unexpected freedom from the long, heavy skirts of earlier years. It was more convenient, especially when women had to work in munitions factories or doing the jobs that men had done before the war. Heavy petticoats and layers of underclothes soon disappeared and women enjoyed the freedom from whalebone corsets and stiff starched cotton underskirts.

Women of all social classes took more care of their appearance, particularly those less well off. They tried to be more neatly dressed and clean their hair, teeth and fingernails. But for many it was still a constant struggle to find any money from the weekly budget for clothes for the children - and the women were always last when it came to new clothes or shoes.

Women also started to wear trousers more frequently. First seen as a fashion statement in the early 1900s, during the war they became practical and warm for women expected to work outside or for those who needed to move about quickly, either in the cities or in the country.

10.3.3. The 1920s

Once women had experienced freedom from the layers of clothing and stiff, heavy clothes they were reluctant to return to them after the war. Even when it was no longer considered patriotic to wear shorter skirts the hemlines remained firmly above the ankle. It was more convenient and comfortable and by 1926 hemlines had risen just above the knee. Changes in standards of clothing for the poor and working class were one of the most obvious signs of improving material conditions. Even among the poor, barefoot women walking the streets and children dressed in rags became something less often seen after the Great War.

The fashion of the 1920s was a 'tubular' look; straight dresses which had no obvious waistline. Light underwear was designed to flatten the bosom and new, lighter fabrics were used for stockings; silk or flesh coloured rayon and nylon.

There was still a great variation of clothes and fashion worn by women. For the poorer women who couldn't afford to buy new clothes whenever the fashions changed, or for the older generation, long, heavy skirts were still worn with a flowered pinafore or housecoat over the top.

Young girls who were earning money for the first time were keen to spend their spare cash on clothes and makeup. The shops springing up in towns and cities were keen to provide what they wanted. Woolworths stocked cheap makeup and beads that, with a light, flowery dress would make any girl feel great, whatever part of society she came from.

10.3.4. The 1930s

The new Duchess of York encouraged women to dress in a very feminine style. Dresses were made of a flowery material, often in chiffon, with frills and bows. Padding was popular to accentuate the shoulders and hats, often in Victorian colours of violet and plum, were adorned with feathers and brooches. The duchess was a fashionable, glamorous woman and thousands of young women followed her style, whatever she wore.

Generally the fashions were freer, lighter and more ambitious. Much use was made of cheaper new fabrics that even a working girl could afford. Cheap copies of dresses worn by prominent, wealthy women, such as the duchess and the new film stars of the cinema, became popular in the new chain stores in London and the provinces. Ready-made clothing became popular as it was cheaper and more readily available. Young women flocked to buy the newest fashions of dresses, trousers, blouses and coats. Hats and jewellery were popular and eventually even the poor started to have a little money to spend on themselves. But as always, there were some for whom even the new cheaper clothes were out of reach. For many the only clothes they could afford were old second- or third-hand dresses from the pawn shop or the rags they already had.

Magazines, newspapers and advertisements encouraged women to be feminine. To look after themselves to keep their husbands interested. As one advertisement put it: 'keep young and beautiful/ it's your duty to be beautiful/ keep young and beautiful - if you want to be loved.'

10.3.5. Hair

Just as clothes underwent changes in fashion, so did hairstyles. At the start of the Edwardian era women wore their hair long, as they had done throughout Victorian times, and wound up into a bun. For those on low incomes there was never time or money for lengthy grooming or trips to a hairdresser. It was even more difficult for those living in the slums and poor tenements where even regular washing was a luxury. But for the wealthy their hair was their crowning glory. They had servants who would dress their hair and keep it in top condition. It was brushed in the morning before being wound up into an impressive mound, or curled with tongs heated in the fire. At night it was brushed again, platted up to keep it from getting tangled and paper ringlets pressed into service to ensure there would be a few curls in the morning.

During the Great War hair styles became much shorter. Women, even wealthy ones, didn't have the time to spend looking after long hair. For those working on a farm or around workplace machinery it was dangerous, even when tied up out of the way. Women found freedom in the short, modern styles of the era.

In the 1920s the fashion was for the 'bob' or 'shingle'. In 1926 the 'Eton Crop' became very popular. The new short hair styles with a short fringe matched the boyish clothes. Generally women wore their hair straight and short. It was much easier and quicker to prepare.

10.3.6. Clothing for the Poor

Whilst there were dramatic changes in clothing for those with a little money in their pockets, for those struggling to find enough money to put food on the table there were few changes. There was nothing left out of the weekly pay packet for clothes.

Overtime at Christmas might pay for clothes or the family might chose to buy them during the summer when there was less money needed for fuel. There were clubs, run by local tradesmen, who allowed a little to be put by each week so that when there was a crisis there would be something available to help; such as material for a new dress or boots for one of the children. Clothes were rarely bought ready-made and never bought new. They would be bought fourth- or fifth-hand off the market stalls or from the pawn shop or material would be bought and a dress or shirt made for the children.

There was an order of priority in the family. The man went out to work and so should never go without. The children must be reasonably dressed when they went to school and so they would take the next priority. There was no such requirement for the woman of the family. She could go out to do what she needed to, shopping or visiting, during the evening when no one would see that she had no boots on her feet or holes in her blouse or shawl. Most poor women had a hat, jacket and a 'best' skirt to wear in the street. In the house a blouse and patched skirt under a sacking apron was usually worn. Some women looked clean and tidy even with so little, but many others didn't.

10.4. Women and Work

At the start of the Edwardian era a woman's place was still very much in the home looking after her husband and children. But, as ever, it was a country of two halves. The well off remained in the home, often having little to do other than make sure that the servants did their work. They would visit ladies in a similar situation as themselves or go shopping or out to luncheon.

For working class women it was very different. It was often necessary for them to bring in a little extra money, especially if the children were at school or out at work. The pennies earned might be the only money she had to spend on food that week. For mothers with a large number of children their work was in the home and it was back breaking work, looking after children, mending and making clothes, cooking, cleaning and carrying water to and from the well or water supply in the back yard. The work was never finished, even once everyone else was in bed at night.

During the war many things changed, not least that women had to work to keep the country running. Even titled ladies living in country mansions started working, many letting their homes become hospitals for the injured and sick from the front. Many of their daughters trained as nurses to tend the sick, others knitted or sewed items to send to soldiers at the front.

Middle- and working-class women had to change their outlook on life. Many young women became just as skilled as their brothers or father when it came to tending the farm, working in the factories or driving trams and lorries. They learned new skills as mechanics, factory and farm workers. They had a new role doing heavy work that had previously been the work of men. Women were needed, working round the clock to ensure that the country still ran and that food and clothing, ammunition and vehicles were sent out to the soldiers at the front and men in the navy.

But at the end of the war the men returning from the front needed their jobs back. There were not enough jobs for the women to carry on working, even with the huge loss of life during the war and during the Influenza epidemic of 1918. Women were expected to return to the role they had played before the war. When the men returned they found their women had changed too.

The number of women employed rose from 3.27 million in 1914 to 4.53 million in 1918. But by November 1919, when all men had been demobilized and returned from the war, 775,000 women lost their jobs. The government claimed it was unpatriotic for any woman to remain in a job if it was needed by a man returning from the war. Pressure was put on women to cultivate their domestic skills again. The post war establishment was anxious to eliminate any threat to the shrinking labour market which the returning men faced.

Many women rebelled; they didn't want to be treated the same way and they petitioned for change. After 1919 women could become solicitors, doctors and accountants. Gradually universities opened their doors to women and degrees were offered.

As the 1920s progressed there were concerns that women were no longer interested in becoming wives and mothers. Politicians worried that they would want to be career women, staying single and enjoying their new freedom. But their fears were groundless; the 1920s saw a rise in the number of marriages and there was an increase in the number of babies being born.

But women had tasted freedom and that was not going to go away. Those who were not interested in following the traditional domestic role for women could choose an alternative; running businesses, joining the professions or simply being independent. But it wasn't easy for them.

During the economic slump of the 1930s thousands of women lost their jobs. The unemployment figures given by the government were inaccurate in that they didn't reflect the number of women who were out of work. Married women were prevented from claiming any benefits and the numbers quoted didn't include them. Any jobs were given to male applicants.

In 1933 Sir Herbert Austin (the motor manufacturer and former MP for Birmingham Kings Norton) declared that all women should be sacked as an effected means of solving the unemployment problem. He wasn't the only one making such claims. Their inability to see the true picture and devastation that unemployment caused is shocking, but perhaps unsurprising.

11.   Men

11.1.   The vote

Whilst women's suffrage of the early twentieth century has been well documented, it shouldn't be forgotten that the vote for men was far from 'one man, one vote' at that time.

At the start of the twentieth century only two out of three men could vote and that was better than it had been a century before. The qualification was that only men who owned or rented houses worth £10 per annum and paid rates, and had resided there for one year, were allowed to vote. This excluded working class men, many middle class men and all women. This was much better than it had been in the past.

In 1900 the creation of the Labour Representation Committee (which was renamed The Labour Party in 1906) aimed to give trade unions a political arm and so grant a say to the other one in three men.

In 1918 the Representation of the People Act, which famously granted women the right to vote for the first time, also gave men over 21, the other one in three men, the right to have a say in who should represent them in Parliament. Working class men now had a voice.

11.2.   Men and Fashion

In men's fashions form followed function and class. A man could be placed into his occupation and class simply by observing what he wore. An artisan in a suit on Sunday, still looked like an artisan. An earl still looked like an upper class gentleman. Their fashions might have changed with the death of the old queen, but most men still wore the same as all the others in his class. They did not want to stand out. Men were not encouraged to be individuals.

But men had to follow the requirements of their time and status in society just as much as women did. In the early 1900s the working man wore dark coloured, baggy trousers with boots, a collarless shirt with long tails which doubled as underwear, a jacket and cloth cap. During their time off work, whatever their job might be, they would dress as smartly as they could, but they would still be working men dressed in their Sunday best. That changed little through the century. Whilst men became slightly better dressed, elderly men still wore the same in 1939 as they had at the turn of the century. But for younger men, things did start to change.

For the better off there was more of a change. They could afford to buy new clothes as the fashions changed. In 1901 the well-off wore stiff collars, starched shirt fronts and 'leather coffins' on their feet.

During the war men who had enlisted were expected to wear uniform, and most did with pride. But they returned to a changed Britain and many wanted to change too.

By the 1920s King George had popularised single-breasted suits, although his habit of creasing trousers down the side in the navy style, rather than the front, didn't catch on. The soft, coloured homburg hat was replacing the hard black or brown bowler and tall silk hat.

The Prince of Wales, the future Edward VIII, was a fashion icon. He pioneered the cutaway collar and Windsor knot. Dressed in Oxford bags, extravagantly coloured Fair Isle pullovers and a classless cloth cap he was soon setting trends all over the world.

By the 1930s a tanned face and arms had come to symbolize outdoor leisure, rather than being seen as the sign of a working man. Exercise was increasing in popularity, as was wearing loose fitting clothes and shorts. Lord Baden Powell, who started the scouting movement, spent the majority of his life in shorts.

But for all the changes that were hitting the fashion world evening wear had unbending rules. There should be a black tie (never white and never pre-tied) with a black evening jacket and black patent shoes not worn for any other occasion. Evening clothes would be worn to dances, dinners, receptions, the opera and the theatre. As the thirties progressed a new tweed look made an appearance. Moss Bross hired out evening wear for those who like to attend social functions but couldn't afford the cost of the necessary outfit.

During the 1930s menswear became less formal. Hats were only worn as protection against the rain or sun and coats were only worn when it was cold. Loose, blousy shirts replaced starched ones and sandals were often worn rather than shoes. Underwear became looser and less constricting. Men could dress with as much individuality as women, but not amongst the middle-class. Business men all appeared in grey suits and trilby hats. But for the younger men who could afford the fashions, they could be as individual as they wanted to be.

A wealthy, professional man would dress in a suit tailored in Saville Row or a small bespoke establishment in another town. Inside leg measurements were taken and much thought given to getting the fitting just right. But the suits were nothing that would turn the eye for anything other than its beautiful fit and style. The less well-off middle-class and working-class man who wanted a 'Sunday best' could buy a suit at Burton or Horne Brothers, at a cost of 50 - 60s (£2 10s - £3).

For the cost conscious, off-the-peg suits were becoming more popular and started to take over from tailor made garments. Shops adapted to these cost and labour saving methods.

By this time teachers, shop assistants and clerks all wore suits to work. Older men would wear a suit to the greyhound track or pub. Younger middle-class men were more likely to wear a sports jacket, knitted cardigan or a hand knitted V-necked sleeveless pullover to hide their braces (which were considered most common). A short sleeved tie-less shirt, flannel trousers or shorts (or plus fours and argyle patterned socks if you really had to).

12.   Religion

The Church has played a major role in the lives of British people from very early in the history of England and Wales. But just because the Church was the centre of the parish did not mean that everyone attended on a Sunday. By the start of the twentieth century its position as the central point in the parish was being usurped.

12.1.   Christianity

The large scale urbanization of the mid- to late-nineteenth century forced the traditional role of the parish into decline. Generally, the larger the population of an area the smaller the reliance on the Church. Large communities no longer needed the dominant role of the church as they had done in small parishes. In urban areas the Church had to compete with cinemas, pubs, football teams, sport and the work place for people's time and attention. There was much more for people in towns and cities to do.

The virtual truth of the bible that had been questioned by Charles Darwin in his books *On the Origin of the Species* in 1859 and *Decent of Man* in 1871 had had a big impact on people's beliefs. The Prince of Wales was often seen to be late to Church and held dinner parties on Sundays, something which a generation before would have been unheard of in someone so prominent.

Whilst people were still keen to get married, have their children baptised and be buried in Churches or chapels, those were increasingly the only times that people went to a church service. Most people in England and Wales, if asked, would confirm that they believed in some sort of God, but that it was not necessary to go to church each week. In 1913 one West Midlands newspaper reported that 'the Church is out of sympathy with the masses.' A feeling echoed around many homes at the time.

Many upper class families went to church each week 'to keep up appearances', but even that was starting to decline.

12.2.   Church of England

The clergy of the Church of England (and Wales) were no longer only taken from younger sons of the upper classes. Many were now training for the Church because they believed that they could make a difference in people's lives. It is hardly surprising that for many their faith was challenged by the First World War. Many lost sons, brothers, friends and parishioners and had to comfort grieving families when they could hardly find comfort themselves. Many started to question the values of the Church as they saw how it had failed to play a major part in the lives of soldiers.

Once the war was over the clergy had to try to keep their parishioners attending services. By the end of the nineteenth century the principle form of growth of church membership was internal, by children and friends joining, rather than by evangelical messages. This was the start of the declining membership numbers. There was the added concern now that the Church no longer reflected the way of life of the majority of people in England and Wales. The Church was becoming less relevant to a modern Britain.

The Church itself was still run by a few very wealthy individuals who obtained their posts because of who they were rather than being voted in because of their beliefs and what they had to offer the membership. The church's lack of democracy was at odds with the modern world, particular the post war world that had fought for democracy in Europe.

Fig 12.1: Meifod Parish Church, Powys. The Parish church was no longer the centre of many people's lives in the early twentieth century.

The desire for reform started with the Life and Liberty movement founded in 1917. Its objective was to increase self-government for the Church. Its aim was for the Church to represent all classes not just the upper classes that had been given a say previously. There was a need for a post war Church that everyone could understand and that worked for all its members. They proposed a democratically elected Church Assembly, equalization of clerical stipends, abolition of the parochial system and a volunteer army of missionaries to re-evangelize the country. By 1920 the more radical ideas had been dropped, but it had left a concern about the Church's place in society and the changes that needed to happen. More clergy were needed and they needed a more stringent training program to prepare them for the ministry. That ministry needed to be based on their faith, not their wealth or place in society.

A School of Instruction in France and one in Knutsford, Cheshire were set up in 1918. These were intended to bring new blood to the clergy to fill the gaps left by retirement, those who no longer wished to practice, and those who had been killed or injured during the war. Enough new clergy were instructed by 1921 to fill the void, but that still left the question of how the Church could best serve the country in the modern world. Change was slow.

12.3.   Roman Catholic

Persecution of Catholics was long passed and there was a strong, though small, membership of the Roman Catholic Church throughout England and Wales. In 1901 there was a membership of two million, which grew steadily throughout the early years of the twentieth century, in contrast to the general decline in church membership. By 1939 membership had reached three million.

One of the ways in which Catholic numbers increased was by the Church's unyielding attitude to mixed marriages, which bought in about 12,000 converts each year. Additionally anyone marrying in a Catholic church had to promise to bring up their children in the Catholic faith.

There was a rapid expansion of Catholic clergy and a forward thinking church building programme, particularly in the new London suburbs. Suburban Kent had 22 new Catholic Churches built during 1930 - 39. There was also an expansion of Catholic public schools and the number of Catholic dons at Oxford and Cambridge Universities during the same years. Their membership was also assisted by the steady stream of Irish Catholic immigrants to the country with a high birth rate.

12.4.   Non-Conformist Chapels

Non-Conformist Chapels throughout England and Wales largely comprised of Baptist, Methodist and Congregationalists. Each had their own chapels, rules, beliefs and ordained their own ministers. A large number of chapels had been built during the nineteenth century, particularly in Wales.

Methodists were formed from an amalgamation of New Connexions, Bible Christians and Free Churches in 1907 to form the United Methodist Church, which in turn joined with the Primitives and Wesleyans in 1932 to reunite all Methodists under one Church.

The Baptist Union was formed in 1891 from the General Baptists and the Particular Baptists which united to form one Church. Their chapels were managed by internal membership, rather than a general synod.

The Congregationalists and Presbyterians (which in 1972 joined to form the United Reformed Church) were Protestants that believed the congregation is autonomous under God, and as such they do not have any church synod or outside elders. They were particularly common in Wales.

There has long been a rivalry between Church and Chapel (of the various denominations). However, the non-conformist churches experienced a drop in membership before the Great War, some years before it was noticed in the Church of England (and Wales).

12.5.   Declining Membership

A fall in membership numbers was seen in all churches across England and Wales in the first half of the twentieth century and beyond. Whilst it paused during the 1920s as people got back to a 'normal' way of life, the decline wasn't stopped. As membership numbers dropped it became apparent that the makeup of the congregation was changing.

As the membership aged it was not being replaced by the children of those who attended. The congregations were getting older. There were few young men under 35 and whilst there were slightly more women and girls, the majority of the congregation were middle aged and elderly people who had attended all their lives.

During the 1930s the Church's authority (both Church of England/Wales and non-conformist) was challenged by social and legal changes. Its doctrines were tested and its importance in many people's lives diminished. Its role in giving clear spiritual and moral guidelines was being reduced by divisions within and by confusion and volatility of politics.

In the 1931 census 60% of the population said they were Church of England, 15% Non-Conformist and 5% Catholic. 'Being Christian' meant someone was baptised, married and buried by the Church and generally lived by a moral code. Some would go to Church at Christmas and Easter, but not otherwise. Far fewer were regular church goers. In 1930 it was estimated that there were 5.5 million (both Church of England and Non-Conformist) and 2.8 million Catholics out of a population of 35 million adults.

Three quarters of the congregation on an ordinary Sunday were women. Even those who rarely went themselves thought it was good that children received religious instruction. It was seen as the best way to impart 'ethical principles'. Sunday Schools were popular throughout this period for this purpose.

Attendance varied across the country. Those in the country were more likely to attend than those who lived in towns. Attendance was lower in the North of England than in the South. In parts of Lancashire and NW England there was a substantial Catholic population. Surveys of Liverpool found that only 15-20% of the population ever went to Church. And the figures were declining.

The higher a person's social class, the more likely they were to go to church. The young and old were more likely to attend, and women more likely to attend than men. The Church still had influence, its leaders were leaders in politics, police, magistrates' benches, local press and business men.

To try to encourage membership, the Pleasant Sunday Afternoon Movement was formed in the midlands and had become a national organisation by 1905. In 1913 there were 329 branches and almost 56,000 members. Their meetings concentrated on music, discussions and informal Christian teaching. It was popular, but it failed to stem the diminishing membership.

12.6. Competition

During the early twentieth century Church membership was highest in rural villages, and lowest in cities and the growing suburbia. The *Methodist Times* summarized working class attitudes after the Great War: 'we don't want your gospel, we want a new social order.' By the 1920s many felt the Church and Chapels no longer reflected the current world.

In the late nineteenth century the Church provided a multitude of leisure and recreational outlets: Boys' Brigade, Girls' Brigade, dances, meetings and outings. These remained prominent in the early twentieth century Edwardian society, but after the Great War things started to change.

In rural areas new forms of entertainment were slow to arrive. Cinemas didn't appear until the 1930s and groups of girls who attended pubs alone were still frowned upon. Dances and outings put on by the Church were still the main form of entertainment and youngsters tended to join the Church just as their parents had done. But in the towns and urban areas social life was much more varied. There were new forms of entertainment not arranged by the church. Cinemas were allowed to show films on Sundays. Dances were arranged in local halls and meeting places. The Church was no longer the centre of everything that people did and Church membership was no longer essential to everyday life. And membership fell accordingly.

The Great War widened people's horizons. Men who enlisted, and many women, had travelled abroad as part of the war effort. Americans came to England and Wales and their different attitude to life soon became apparent. Women and young people had money of their own, many for the first time in their lives. People saw that there was another way to live and they liked what they saw. England and Wales changed forever.

Working patterns changed too. A half day holiday on Saturday and reduced working hours during the week saw the traditional 'Sabbath' subsumed by the modern secular 'weekend'. Shops might be closed but pubs, cinemas and seaside resorts were open and vied for business. The Sunday afternoon drive was well established by the late 1930s. For many Sunday became a day for domestic activities: gardening, home improvements and hobbies.

12.7.   Outdated

The opposition of the Church to divorce played a critical role in the abdication of Edward VIII in 1936. It was also opposed to the work of Marie Stopes to popularise artificial contraception. In Wales in 1927 attempts to play golf in Aberdyfi led to players being physically threatened. Yet Parliament was still opened by prayers and the Annual Remembrance Day Service was a national event. For many people of working- and middle-class the Church was outdated and no longer reflected their views on life or how they wanted to live. It was easier to not attend church and enjoy life, rather than try to change such a huge organisation that many believed had never listened to their views.

13.   Events during 1901 - 1939

13.1.   Wars

England and Wales suffered two wars during the years 1901 to 1939. There are hundreds of books written about these wars, but here are just a few points that will have affected those who lived through this time.

13.1.1. The Boer War 1899 - 1901

In comparison with the Great War, the Boer War is less well known, but it was still expensive (costing £200 million) and bloody (56,000 allied troops died, as did tens of thousands of men, women and children from the region) and should not be forgotten. This is just a snapshot of what happened and how it affected the British at home.

13.1.1.1.   What Happened

The Boers were white farmers, whose ancestors (Dutch, Huguenot and German immigrants) had settled the Cape area of South Africa in 1652. In 1814 the British took control of the area, but 10,000 Boers (Dutch for 'farmer') refused to submit to foreign colonial rule and left the Cape to embark on the 'Great Trek' of 1835-42. They moved north to Natal and set up two republics; the Orange Free State and the South African (Transvaal Republic).

There had already been one Boer War (or First Freedom War as the South African's refer to it) in 1880-81, but that failed to finish matters to the Boers' satisfaction. On 11th October 1899 they declared war on Britain (their Second Freedom War) and invaded the Cape Colony, north Natal and besieged the garrison towns of Ladysmith and Mafeking. The British defended what they saw as their territory and countries throughout the Empire sent troops to form the British Imperial Force. Whilst the British did have some victories in battles at Talana and Elansalaagte, there were serious defeats at Stromberg, Magersfontein and Colenso in what became known as the 'black week', 10 - 15 December 1899.

With heavy reinforcements the British turned the situation around. Imperial troops relieved the towns of Ladysmith (28 February 1900), Kimberley (15 February 1900) and Mafeking (18 May 1900). On 13 March 1900 the British Imperial Force captured Bloemfontein (the capital of the Orange Free State) and renamed it Orange River Colony. On 31st May 1900 British troops entered Johannesburg and on 5th June Pretoria was taken. Believing that the war was over, Roberts, the head of the Imperial Forces, returned to England in triumph.

But the Boers had not finished fighting. They were a civilian militia; each man chose what to wear, usually grey, black or earth tone khaki farming clothes comprising jacket, trousers and slouch hat. Most Boers were not war hungry. They did not look forward to fighting fellow Christians, but many believed that it was a holy and just war.

The Boers changed tactics and adopted a guerrilla style that used small military units. Those units captured supplies, disrupted communications and made raids on the occupying forces, slipping through British lines to evade capture. In response the British adopted a scorched earth policy to deny supplies to the Boers. 30,000 farms were burnt and thousands of families displaced. To restrict the movement of the Boers 8,000 blockhouses were built to secure supply routes, with 6 - 8 soldiers guarding each one. 50,000 troops, 50 battalions, were involved in blockhouse duty. In addition 16,000 Africans were used as armed guards and for patrols at night.

3,700 miles of thick barbed wire fencing stretched between each blockhouse. The British used this to corner the Boers, but it also caught thousands of displaced Boer and African families. Refugees were sent to concentration camps in South Africa. The British set up 45 tented camps for Boer internees and 64 for Black Africans. There were 28,000 male Boer prisoners of which 25,630 were sent to camps overseas. The local camps housed the women and children. It is believed that 26,000 died during their internment in these camps.

The death of so many prisoners was largely caused by poorly administered and overcrowded camps. There was inadequate shelter for the thousands held there and there was a poor and inadequate diet, inadequate hygiene and the inmates suffered from malnutrition and endemic contagious diseases. The shortage of modern medicines compounded the problem and caused the death of tens of thousands of people.

It was these horrific statistics that were largely responsible for bringing the Boers to the negotiating table in 1901, which in turn brought an end to the war.

On May 31st 1901 conditions of surrender were signed in the form of the Treaty of Vereeniging. The two republics were absorbed into the British Empire with the promise of self-government in the future. That promise was fulfilled when the Union of South Africa was created in 1910.

At the end of the war the terrible cost, both in lives lost and in financial terms, became apparent. The horrifying statistics shocked Britons back home and people across the Empire.

55,000 British soldiers had been killed, died, captured or wounded. 10,000 British soldiers died as a result of combat, 12,000 from disease and one was eaten by a crocodile. 25,000 African lives were also lost. The losses were compounded by the poor physical condition of British troops and their lack of knowledge about the environment they were fighting in. Their poor training in the tactical conditions of the war meant that men struggled from the outset.

Soldiers from across the Empire fought with the British Imperial Force. 7,000 Canadian soldiers and support personnel, of which 270 soldiers died. 6,500 volunteers and 8,000 horses came from New Zealand plus doctors, nurses, vets and a small number of school teachers. 70 died and 158 were killed by disease or accident. 24,000 South Africans fought with the British Imperial Forces, hundreds of whom were killed. And 20,000 served from Australia, of which 16,443 were enlisted men and 7,000 irregulars were raised in South Africa. Of these 500 irregulars lost their lives, 267 died of disease, 251 killed in action and 43 reported missing.

There were also a huge number of horses killed during the fighting. The average life expectancy of a horse once it had arrived in Port Elizabeth was just six weeks. This was because they were overloaded with equipment and saddles, given too little rest, poor management and poor food.

13.1.1.2.   At Home

At the outbreak of the war there had been public support. The Conservatives rose to a landslide victory on the strength of wars won during the nineteenth century and the public were sure this would be another quick victory. But the losses mounted and as time went on public support waned.

Emily Hobhouse visited the concentration camps in January 1901 and brought home news and photographs of the appalling conditions suffered by those held there. The public were horrified, both at these images and at the scorched earth policy that had forced the clearance of women and children, destroyed their homesteads and poisoned wells. Images of children made homeless by the war, lying seriously malnourished, little more than skeletons, raised fury in Britain.

But for the generals the 154,000 Boer and African citizens in concentration camps were a low priority against the overall military objectives and the voices of dissent were ignored. In 1900 the conservatives found themselves on the receiving end of that fury. At the general election they suffered a landslide defeat, with the public demanding that something should be done.

13.1.1.3.   The Aftermath

One of the lasting effects of the Boer War was concern at the poor condition of recruits. Up to 60% (although some figures show only 34%) of volunteers for the army failed to meet the required standards for height, weight and eyesight. This strengthened the belief that the condition of the poor and their living conditions needed urgent investigation.

The lessons learned during the Boer War meant that the British were able to gear up much faster for the Great War that was to follow just twelve years later.

13.1.2. The Great War 1914 - 1918

There are many excellent books about the Great War. This is a very brief overview of the effect it had on those who lived through those turbulent years.

13.1.2.1.   Abroad

In one week during September 1914 175,000 men volunteered for the armed forces and by the end of that month almost 750,000 men had come forward. By the time conscription was introduced in March 1916 over 2.5 million men had volunteered and been mobilised. Even taking into consideration the 16,000 conscientious objectors, by the end of the war one in three adult males had undergone military service.

Once men had signed up for the duration of the war they were sent for a brief period of training. Once that was completed they were moved and could end up anywhere, but often it was to France and Belgium on the Western Front. They ended up in sodden, filthy trenches, where there were the joint horrors of enemy fire, disease and drowning. Some wondered whether disease and the weather were on the German side, until they realised that the Germans had the same problems as the Allies.

In the Battles at the Western and Eastern Fronts millions of men were injured and killed. Those that survived lived through horrific battles and had to suffer the memory of the horrors of mutilation, death and drowning.

By the end of the war in November 1918, 750,000 men, almost 9% of all men under 45 in Britain, had been killed. A further 1.6 million had been wounded. The majority were middle class officers and working class men. Hospital trains arrived regularly at Victoria and Charring Cross Stations to bring the wounded to emergency hospitals that had been set up in schools, warehouses and country houses. Women were hurriedly trained as nurses, many of whom had come from privileged lives, never having worked before.

But during the entire war, whatever the conditions on the ground were, there were no serious mutinies of consequence in the British Army. Morale may have buckled at times, but it never broke. Soldiers grumbled, swore, ate bully beef, drank tea and plodded on. The camaraderie in the trenches made it bearable. Friendships, many of which lasted a life time back at home, were formed. Extraordinary acts of bravery were recorded.

Many soldiers hoped for a slight injury; a 'Blighty one'; not serious but enough to see them heading for home. But there was an acceptance that if a bullet 'had your name on it' there was nothing you could do. Men endured, suffered and many died. But they never gave up.

Few families escaped death or injury to a father, son, brother, uncle or cousin. Some families fared worse than others. After the war the sight of a disabled man, with a missing limb or vacant stare, was common enough on streets around England and Wales in towns and villages alike.

13.1.2.2.   At Home

At the start of the war the country moved to gear the economy towards the needs of its army and navy. Factories were taken over to manufacture arms and munitions, railways and mines taken under government control. By March 1918 the government had taken ownership of 250 mines and quarries.

The mass enlistment of men into the army and navy had led to huge labour shortages. One fifth of miners joined up in the first year of the war and by 1915 recruiting officers were advised not to accept men from certain occupations and skilled men were brought back from the front.

There was a drop in unemployment, from 2.4% in June 1914 to 0.5% by August 1918, and a reduction in the number of paupers. By July 1918 the number was two thirds of what it had been in July 1914.

In August 1915 a National Census was held. From this a National Register was compiled of all men and women aged 15 - 65 who could help with the war effort. It was found that by the end of 1915 only 1.15 million, out of 2.18 million available single men, had enlisted. Conscription was inevitable.

Strikes by employees became illegal from 1915, but they did occasionally happen. Workers in Clydeside held a strike in March 1916 and in Coventry in November 1917, but these were short and workers were soon back in their posts. One of the most serious was a miners strike in South Wales in July 1915. Because of the consequence and effect of the strike the government got involved and the strikers' demands were met after just five days. Miners were needed to work, not strike. But industrial unrest became worse in 1917, largely because of the number of unskilled workers who were being used to fill jobs that needed skilled workers; which the unions referred to as dilution. This happened mostly in firms that were not engaged directly in war work.

The majority of the unrest was because of the high cost of food. Wages had increased, but that increase was less than inflation and the high cost of living and people were struggling. Those struggling to make ends meet weren't any better off. It wasn't until the war ended and food restrictions were lifted that people were any better off.

One of the most noticeable things about life at home during the war was the greater amount of government regulation (see section 7.2.2.2), which people were not used to. Restrictions in pub licensing hours, additional taxation, food restrictions and material and clothes allowance all affected morale and public spirit.

Whilst the majority of casualties were on the Eastern and Western Fronts abroad, not all people at home were out of harm's way and soon measures were taken to lessen the likelihood of attacks from the Continent. Blackouts were imposed because of the fear of Zeppelin raids. London was hit on 8th October 1915 when 38 were killed and 87 injured. There were 51 raids by Zeppelins and 57 by aeroplanes during the war which killed and injured 4,820 people. Coastal attacks from German warships in December 1914 on Hartlepool, Whitby and Scarborough injured still more. Dover suffered cross-channel shelling throughout the war. Civilian casualties amounted to 5,611 including 1,570 deaths, all but 157 of them being in air raids.

13.2. Customs, Fairs and Holidays

Britain has held fairs and celebrations at different times of the year since medieval times. In the past they were linked to the seasons of the year and many of these are still celebrated today. Many secular festivals held since medieval times have been amalgamated into the Christian calendar and now have religious significance. Whatever the occasion people were keen to celebrate. It was a chance to leave the hardships of work and poverty behind, even if just for a few hours.

13.2.1. Christmas

They way Christmas has been celebrated has changed considerably over the years. Today's commercial frenzy is a very modern invention that had its roots in the early twentieth century. By 1920 it was common to see small gifts being left beneath the Christmas tree in the parlour on Christmas morning. Historically it was a time for festivals, mumming plays and Yuletide celebrations, although very few mumming plays would have been seen at the start of the century.

The run up to Christmas started early when puddings and cakes were made. Children helped stone the raisins, cutting each one, taking out the stone and washing it in hot water. Almonds were 'blanched' and skinned by dipping the nut in hot water and letting the skin slide off in their fingers.

Christmas puddings were made from the fruit and dry ingredients being mixed with porter (a mild type of beer) in a very large mixing bowl. Silver 'thru'penny bits' were added and then each person in the family would stir the mixture for luck. Once it had stood overnight to blend the flavours it was put into china pudding basins (or copper ones if the family had them) and steamed over boiling water for eight hours. Often the family would also make pickled red cabbage and green walnuts, salt-beef and sweets. Everything would be tucked away for Christmas day.

Decorations were made by the family. Coloured paper-chains were made by cutting strips of coloured paper or card and sticking them together with flour and water paste. They would then be hung round the parlour or family room. Christmas cards and carols were common by this time and by 1910 Father Christmas was almost universally seen in his red suit (before then it might be red, green or blue) as he and Saint Nicholas had been merged. 1912 saw the first display of lights being opened by Princess Louise. It was 'festoons of garland lamps' which included 10,000 light bulbs.

Christmas trees were popularised by Prince Albert and the Royal Family in the nineteenth century. Since then many families enjoyed decorating a tree and giving and receiving small gifts. In the early twentieth century real trees would be cut down and brought inside on Christmas Eve, amidst the smell of pine cones and wood. The *Book of Home* explained how children and adults could decorate them with paper garlands and coloured glass baubles, sweets, toys and dolls.

On Christmas Eve children hung stockings on the end of their beds, or on the chimney breast and would awake on Christmas morning to find them filled with sweets, nuts, an orange or apple and small gifts and a bright new penny (if their parents could afford them).

Christmas morning was a time for family. Children would open their stockings and there would be a meal of meat with all the trimmings. Birds, such as turkey or chicken, were not often eaten as they were sold by butchers with heads and feathers still on them and the family would have to prepare them for eating, not a pleasant job. Pork was a popular choice. Beef was eaten during the rest of the year so it would be avoided at Christmas time in order to have something different.

Most of the festivities and celebrations would have revolved around the church during the 1901 - 1939 period with services on Christmas Eve and Christmas Day.

Boxing Day was a day to visit relatives, with singing round the piano and indoor games, such as charades, played with cousins, aunts and uncles.

13.2.2. Plough Monday (first Monday after the Twelfth Night) January.

Plough boys and Morris dancers went around the villages dancing and collecting money for feasting and drinking before the start of the agricultural year. This had become less common as there were fewer men and women working on the land, but the celebration would still have been seen in some villages and rural areas at the start of the twentieth century.

13.2.3. Shrove Tuesday

Traditionally this was a day of pancakes and carnivals, with football played in the streets before the sombre days of Lent. Street football had largely disappeared by the start of the twentieth century with the increase in the number of motor vehicles and the imposition of strict rules and specific places to play sport. But Shrove Tuesday was still a big celebration with the extent and exuberance of carnivals varying across the country.

13.2.4. Mid Lent Sunday

This was a holiday for servant girls, when they would traditionally be given a day off work to visit their mother. At the start of the century servant girls could be found in every town, city, village and county. But as the century progressed the numbers dropped and fewer would have taken this holiday.

13.2.5. Easter

In the past this was a time when fairs and games were held in celebration of spring. As the twentieth century progressed the celebrations changed. Easter was generally the earliest point in the year when fairs could be held, as before that days would be too short and cold. By the time spring arrived everyone was happy to throw off the chills of winter and celebrate. By the early twentieth century the Christian celebration and the pagan festival of new life had merged into one.

Celebrating with chocolate eggs is a recent tradition; Nestle made their first chocolate eggs in 1914. Before this chocolate was usually shaped as fish (because of the Bible story telling how Jesus ate fish with his disciples after the resurrection) and chickens (Christ foretold that once Judas had betrayed him the cock would crow). Easter eggs were developed as they represented new life and renewal, something that had been celebrated for centuries. It was only during the 1920s that chocolate eggs were made using moulds. However, they were expensive and were not something that many people could afford.

At the start of the century church services would have formed the focal point of Easter, both on Good Friday and Easter Day, but that wouldn't stop the celebrations from taking place at the fairs held in the streets of towns and villages.

13.2.6. May Day

This was a festival of youth, with garlands, may dolls, May Poles and dancing. In earlier years this was often merged with Oak Apple Day (commemorating Charles II's escape after the battle of Worcester) but it is unlikely this would still have been celebrated at the start of the century. However, May Day celebrations together with big fairs remained popular throughout England.

The May Pole was a tall wooden pole with coloured ribbons fixed to the top. The dancers, dressed in traditional costumes, danced around the pole, weaving in and out of each other holding onto the ribbons. As they did so the ribbons made a pattern down the pole. Different dances made different patterns, with the dancers having to get closer to the pole and each other as the ribbons wound round. Once the ribbons were too short to dance with the dancers would turn the other way and dance their way outward again, unravelling the ribbons as they went.

13.2.7. Whitsun (late May)

This was a late may celebration, with ales, revels, sports, dancing and fairs.

13.2.8. Harvest

Celebrated with a procession as the last cartload of corn was brought into the barn, followed by feasting and dancing into the night. There would be Church services to celebrate the harvest in cities and towns, but for the most part the celebrations would be amongst the rural folk whose lives depended upon the success of the harvest each year.

13.2.9. Hallowe'en (end October)

A night when evil spirits were exorcised before the dark nights of winter. This celebration had an almost mythical reverence and in recent times it has been reinvented. But in the times when people were more superstitious this holiday held special and important significance.

By the start of the twentieth century people were starting to become more secular particularly in towns and cities. The traditional celebrations are more likely to have been held in rural areas where people retained their superstitions.

13.2.10.   Fifth November

Anti-Catholic sermons rang out when people celebrated the triumph of Protestantism with bonfires and fireworks. Although the strict religious significance of the date had disappeared by the early 1900s, the use of bonfires and fireworks has long continued.

13.2.11.   Customs

Customs and practices of these celebrations would have varied from village to village and from county to county. The saint's day of the village church would also have been celebrated and it would have been the high point of the year with festivals and carnivals. These celebrations mitigated the harshness of daily life. They were times when people could act in a way that their needs and work wouldn't otherwise allow them to. Many of the celebrations were confined to village and country life and didn't transfer to the cities and towns when the people migrated.

13.2.12.   Fairs

Fairs during the early nineteenth century were big events that drew together everyone, old and young, town and country dweller alike. There would have been peddler's stalls, puppet shows, musicians and menageries, human and animal curiosities, dancing, fighting and drinking. Many of the earlier blood thirsty sports of fisticuffs, boxing, bear baiting and cock fighting had disappeared, but that didn't mean that people didn't know how to have fun.

13.3.   Tragedies

The period of 1901 - 1939 had its share of disasters, over and above the disaster of the Great War. Here are just three that would have affected people in England and Wales, whether directly or indirectly.

This was a period when people were literate and had a little money in their possession. They would have had access to newspapers, which reached large circulations during this period, and some would also have listened to the radio. Newsreels at the cinema became common during this time, when pictures and information would have brought the later disasters to them in a far more personal way than earlier disasters. It didn't matter whether people lived in the towns and villages directly involved or whether they lived at the opposite end of the country, they would have heard about these disasters when they happened or very soon afterwards. There is little doubt that they would have discussed them with their families and friends.

13.3.1. The Sinking of the *RMS Titanic*

On 15th April 1912 a new ship, which very few people had heard about when it first set sail, sank on her maiden voyage, taking with it more than 1500 people, including many of the world's most wealthy men. The enormity of the tragedy and its repercussions made global news. There could have been few people who hadn't heard of the ship by the end of that month.

13.3.1.1.   What Happened

The story of the *Titanic* is well known throughout the western world, with its class distinctions and the 'women and children first' attitude that condemned many men and third class passengers to the icy depths.

The maiden voyage started from Southampton on 10th April 1912. From there the *Titanic* sailed to Queenstown, Ireland to pick up more passengers. Then it was due to sail across the North Atlantic towards New York. However, when only 2,000 miles (3,300km) into the planned journey of 3,300 miles (5,300km) it hit an iceberg. *Titanic* was holed below the water line and in less than three hours the ship had sunk to the bottom, over three kilometres below. The lifeboats, which would hold only 1,200 of the 2,224 people on board, were launched without their full capacity and only 710 people were saved. Many of those who died did so from exposure in the freezing sea. Others drowned as the ship went down.

One terrible aspect of this disaster was the difference that wealth made in the likelihood of survival. 83% of first- and 100% of second-class children were saved. But only 34% of third class children lived. Of the women on board 97% of first- and 86% of second-class were saved, whereas only 46% of third class made it back to port. The men and crew fared even worse. 33% of first- and 8% of second-class men lived, as did just 16% of third-class men and 22% of the crew. In all, less than a third of the passengers and crew survived the disaster. Some survivors died shortly afterwards, from their injuries and the effects of the icy cold sea.

Only 333 bodies were recovered. Some sank with the ship, others were carried away by the strong ocean currents. Several search ships were immediately dispatched to recover the dead, but only one in five were recovered for burial. Of those, many of the third class passengers and crew were buried at sea, a lack of embalming fluid making it impossible for their bodies to be landed at port, health regulations insisting on only embalmed bodies being returned.

13.3.1.2.   Towns Affected

40% of the ship's crew came from Southampton, not only firemen and stokers but stewardesses, victuallers, chefs and galley staff. There were also bakers, butchers, fishmongers, laundrymen, waiters, bed-makers and a printer from the town. In all 350 people. Many had never travelled by boat before, lured to the sea by the glamour and opulence of the ship.

The *Titanic* had been built in Belfast, Ireland, where other crew members came from. At the time of its construction, Harland and Wolff employed 15,000 workers. Both *Olympic* and *Titanic* were constructed at much the same time, the biggest ships ever built.

During the construction of the *Titanic* injuries to the workforce were common and six deaths occurred on the ship itself and two more on the docks and sheds alongside. 246 injuries were recorded, 28 of them severe, such as severed arms and crushed legs.

In both towns there are memorials to the people who died in the disaster.

13.3.1.3.   Newspapers

The first that people would have heard of the sinking and the tragedy was when the news reached the newspapers. Initially the news coming through was fragmented and inaccurate. The press made much of the millionaires lost at sea, but those in steerage (third class) were hardly mentioned. The Daily Mail's headlines on 16th April 1912 were 'Everyone Safe' and 'Helpless giant being towed to port by Allan Liner'. Few column inches were given to the disaster in the local newspapers over and above the statement that the ship had been involved in an accident.

The Sheffield Evening Telegraph of 15th April 1912 stated that 'A New York telegram says it confirmed that the *Titanic* is proceeding to Halifax under her own steam, and that all the passengers are safe. A wireless telegraphic message which has been received in New York from the *Olympic* reports that 20 boatloads of the *Titanic*'s passengers have been transhipped to the Allen Liner *Parisian* and other passengers to the Cunarder *Carpathian*.'

By the end of the following day news had started trickling through that people had died, but the true enormity of what had happened was still to break. The Derby Daily Telegraph of the 16th April stated 'Town in Mourning. Another ray of hope was held out late last night when the wireless operator at Sable Island, when asked as to the possibility of delivering messages to the *Titanic*'s passengers, answered that it would be difficult as the passengers are believed to be dispersed among several vessels'.

But the paper's second edition held different news: 'At 2 o'clock this afternoon the latest news of the *Titanic* disaster indicated that 675 passengers and 200 of the crew had been saved. There is no information as to the remaining 1300 persons on board and unofficially it is feared the latter have perished.' The report went on to say that the only hope was that they had been saved by ships that didn't have wireless telegraphy.

There were reported to be distressing scenes at the White Star Line's headquarters in London and their offices in Southampton where relatives and friends of the crew waited, desperate for information and news. But it would be four days before a list of survivors was available.

By the 17th April news had come through that the Parisian had no survivors on board. On the Wednesday the commander of the *Olympic* sent word that the *Virginian* and *Tunisian* had no survivors either.

By that time the news reported in the newspapers was that the *Titanic* had hit an iceberg travelling at 18 knots and that the shock 'ripped the sides and shattered the bow' and that 'tons of ice fell on the decks'.

By Monday 20th April the story was headline news on almost every newspaper in Britain. The papers vied to be the first to publish survivors' accounts of the disaster, some national papers even trying to get reporters on board the *Carpathian* before it docked in New York on 18th April.

By 26th April there were appeals launched to help the widows and orphans of those who lost their lives in the disaster. In Britain the relief fund totalled almost £450,000 and was only wound up in the 1960s.

13.3.1.4.   How it would have affected people

Those with relatives and friends on board would have waited with dread for news. But for the majority of people in Britain the story would have broken slowly. When the news finally filtered through that the ship had indeed sunk, and had taken some 1500 people with it, it would have been a major news story around the country (and indeed the world). There would have been few people who hadn't heard about the tragedy.

Newspapers made the story headline news as the gathering enormity of it spread. A film, *Saved from Titanic*, was released just 29 days after the disaster. It starred Dorothy Gibson, a silent film actress, who was herself a survivor of the disaster.

The story remained in the news for weeks, which showed the level of interest the public had in the stories from the ship. News of millionaires who had died, and people who survived against all the odds, were covered daily. But in all the thousands of words printed about the disaster, those in third class (steerage) who had boarded the ship hoping for a new life in America, hardly received a mention.

13.3.2. Spanish Flu Epidemic

In June 1918, whilst the world was still struggling with the Great War, a new killer started to emerge. It was a virus that had originated in chickens, mutated to pigs and finally crossed to humans. It took hold of troops stationed in trenches, on ships and in camps and spread quickly. Mild at first, it became known as the three-day sickness. The symptoms were shivering, a sore throat and then a fever. When men and women returned home to Britain after the war they bought the virus with them.

13.3.2.1.   What Happened

The first recorded case was in America, when a cook reported sick. The first wave was mild, with only a few cases ending in death. However, by October 1918 the virus had mutated into a much more deadly one.

Those who caught the illness started with a shivery twinge. Within a few hours their breathing had become difficult and their skin had turned a vivid lavender colour; this was heliotrope cyanosis, a lack of oxygen in the blood. Sufferers would complain of agonizing sore throats, sweats and uncontrollable vomiting. Death followed not long afterwards. The time between the first symptoms and death was typically less than twelve hours.

About one fifth of those infected developed serious side effects; pneumonia or septicaemia. This was before antibiotics and either of them were a death sentence.

This was unlike ordinary seasonal flu, which attacked thousands each winter. That would typically affect the elderly, the weak and sick. This new flu attacked those who should have been the strongest. Those in the age range of 15 - 40 years old. It would seem that the older population had built up immunity from a previous severe flu outbreak in 1880. It was the younger generation, who had no immunity, who were most affected.

13.3.2.2.   Places affected

This flu virus swept across the world, killing millions as it went. It is believed that 550,000 Americans, 150,000 British, 44,000 Canadians, 375 Italians and 450,000 Russians were killed during the summer months of 1918. Complete Eskimo villages were wiped out in the Arctic and 500,000 in Mexico lost their lives.

Worldwide, five times more people were killed by this flu virus than had been killed by the Great War.

13.3.2.3.   The Newspapers

Because the newspapers were still severely restricted in what they could publish, they were not permitted to print anything that would cause mass panic or adversely affect morale. France, Germany, Britain and America were all subject to these restrictions and so the papers concentrated on those affected in Spain, a neutral country and so not subject to restrictions. Because it appeared to the public that Spain was initially the only country affected it became known as the Spanish Flu.

13.3.2.4.   How it Affected People

150,000 people in Great Britain were killed by the virus and more than a fifth of the population were infected during an 18 month period. Almost no family escaped having a member of the family ill with, or having died of, the illness. Businesses lost members of staff, some highly trained whilst others were the ones that made the business successful. In the newspapers during 1918 there were hundreds of 'Wanted' adverts looking for workers to fill positions left vacant by those who had died. Cooks, servants, administrators and nannies. All in great demand.

During the worst waves of the illness there were no grave diggers to bury the dead. There were no nurses or doctors to tend the sick and hospitals were overcrowded. Fourth and fifth year medical students in London were taken out of their classes and used to man hospitals. Women were brought in to tend the sick, many having had no nursing training at all. Most of the qualified nurses and doctors, those who hadn't succumbed to the disease, were still abroad at the front tending the sick and wounded there.

Hospitals were already full of wounded and sick soldiers brought back from the war. There was little room for the hundreds of people in each town who had been infected with flu. Schools, theatres and many shops were closed; either there were no staff to run them or people kept away for fear of infection.

Doctors dispensed conflicting advice; some said to avoid alcohol entirely, others recommended taking a hot toddy and very hot bath before retiring to bed for the night. Some recommended light wine and port. Other doctors advocated the use of tobacco as it was thought to be a form of disinfectant, but others thought it would exacerbate the illness. In the confusion and with a lack of convincing guidance many people resorted to tried and tested age-old remedies; laudanum, opium, quinine, rhubarb, treacle and vinegar were all believed to have healing powers.

Whole classes of children, kept away from school by frightened parents, could be heard playing in the streets, singing: 'I had a little bird/ its name was Enza/ I opened the Window/ and in-flew-Enza.'

There were stories of those who overcame the illness. Winston Churchill's wife Clementine and their youngest daughter Marigold survived as did the King of Spain. However the King of Sweden's youngest son died of the illness and it was widely reported in the newspapers.

The flu cases ended as abruptly as they started. By late 1919 the number of cases had dropped to a handful and people, scarred by war and infection, could start the unenviable task of picking up their lives in a post war Britain.

13.3.3. Gresford Colliery Disaster

On the 22nd September 1934 one of the Britain's worst mining disasters killed 266 people and left 800 children fatherless. Hundreds lost friends, colleagues, school friends, brothers, cousins, husbands and uncles. The whole town was affected. The accident paved the way to new standards in safety and the fund to assist widows and children of the deceased was still running decades later. But those who suffered in the fire more than 2.25 km underground (1.75 miles) never ended their shift or saw daylight again.

13.3.3.1.   What happened?

At 2 o'clock in the morning on 22nd September 1934 there was an explosion 1.75 miles underground in a mine where over 450 men and boys were working. 200 managed to escape to safety, but for those working in the part of the mine where the underground explosion took place, the Dennis Main Deep, there was no escape.

Miner James Brewin, working on his back in the pit when the explosion took place, described the noise as like thunder. The roof only a foot or two above his head cracked and large lumps of coal fell onto him. He scrambled to his knees and pulled himself 'inch by inch to the end of the gallery and then staggered into the cage and was hauled to safety'. He was one of over 200 who escaped with their lives. Another young miner escaped by climbing up an air shaft, barely wide enough to admit his body. However, for those who stayed behind hoping for rescue it was not to arrive.

A large group of rescuers, miners who had escaped and miners waiting for their next shift went below ground in an attempt to rescue those trapped. They were met with 'a wall of flames' three-quarters of a mile down and didn't manage to go any deeper. Any miners below that level died either by the flames or the poisonous gasses that had enveloped much of the mine.

Only a few bodies were recovered. Most of the miners who died were believed to be trapped, held behind rock falls which entombed them. Their bodies were never recovered and the mine remains their grave.

13.3.3.2.   The Newspapers

Understandably, newspapers were full of news of the fire and collapse, although initially the full scale of the human tragedy was unknown. The 'Sunderland Echo', which carried a full front page article on Saturday 22nd September 1922, played on the heroic rescues that had been made. They stated that there had only been six charred bodies brought to the surface and that 100 men were unaccounted for. Their reporter spoke to miners who knew the mine well. One man said that it would take well over a week to get to the deeper part where most of the men were trapped. He held out little hope for their survival.

They also reported that the fire service had raced to the mine when they were notified of the disaster, but that they could only stand and wait, as helpless as the women who stood waiting for news of their husbands, sons and fathers. The fire service waited until eight o'clock that night and then returned to their station in Wrexham. There was nothing they could do to help.

Those who were able to help were the colliery brigadesmen who went down the pit to fight the flames and every available ambulance man in the district who was called to the scene. The manager of the colliery and prominent officials of the company who owned the mine all went below ground to try to help those trapped.

The newspapers told how there were more men underground than there should have been. The 'Lincolnshire Echo' reported (as did most other papers) that there were men and their sons who had changed their shift so that they could go to watch a football match on the Saturday afternoon. The match went ahead, as a tribute to those who had perished.

By the Monday (September 24th) the full extent of the tragedy was known. The Prince of Wales (later King Edward VIII) led the way and donated £100 to a new fund to help the widows and orphans of the tragedy. The Prince and Princess of Greece gave £10 and wealthy men and women across the country soon followed their example. The Bristol 'Western Daily Press' on 26th September carried an appeal by the Lord Mayor for funds to help those bereaved. Other papers across the country carried similar appeals.

On the 28th September the Western Times carried an article stating that the fires still raged in the mines and that there had been no option but to seal the mine head. They further reported on an inquest of a man who had died down the pit whose body had been recovered: 'in the same building where the inquest was held scores of women, most of them in deep mourning and some with children in their arms, were waiting to make their claims to the relief committee which is sitting daily for the purpose of distributing assistance to the sufferers by the disaster.'

13.3.3.3.   How it would have affected people

Hundreds of women and children were left without the breadwinner of the family. This was a poor community in North Wales, where for many the husband was the only breadwinner. Their existence was from day to day. They might have had a small insurance policy to cover the funeral arrangements, but there wouldn't have been savings for them to fall back on. For many, without their husband to bring home his weekly pay, they would have no means of paying their rent or for food for their children. As well as the grief of losing their husband, they would also have the worry of having no money. Some families lost both father and son, both of whom would be bringing in money to the family. The loss would be hard to bear.

The relief fund did provide help, but it was not likely to have been generous or provide support for very long. Women would have to get on with their lives. A second marriage was unlikely unless they moved away from the town, because so many men had lost their lives. Some would marry again, but most would have to find work to keep their children from starvation and the workhouse.

In some cases children were sent away to relatives in adjoining villages where they would be looked after, either long or short term. Families were split up. Friends were suffering too and, although they would want to help, most were in the same situation.

It was not only the families of those who died who were suffering. Women who still had their family around them would have to watch as their father, husband or son went off to work down the mine on their next shift. They must have wondered whether they too would suffer the same fate.

It wasn't just the fire and collapse of the mine shaft that broke families apart. Within a month 1,100 men had signed on for unemployment benefit. The disaster had forced one of the mine's two pit heads on the site to be capped and closed. Half of those employed at the mine lost their jobs.

14.   Further Information

14.1.   Coinage, Weights and Measures

14.1.1. Coinage

During the first half of the twentieth century the British system of money and weights was very different to that which we have today.

Money was based on the British pound (£ or L) which comprised of 20 shillings (s). There were 240 pennies (d) in the pound. A shilling was worth 12 pence (d). Each coin was of a different design although they all featured the head of the monarch on one side and the year the coin was minted on the other.

In order of value the coins were as follows:

- **Farthing:** Worth one quarter of one penny (¼d). This was a small bronze coin, 20mm diameter;

Fig 14.1 Farthing 1921

Half penny: Worth one half of one penny (½d). A bronze coin 26mm diameter;

Fig 14.2 Half Penny 1935

- **Penny:** One Penny (1d). There were 240 pennies in the pound. A bronze coin 31mm diameter;

Fig 14.3: One Penny Piece 1921

- **Three pence**: 3d. Known as 'thropenny bit'. Before 1937 it was a silver coin, 16mm diameter. After that date it was a bronze 12 sided coin, 16mm diameter.

Fig 14.4: 1939 Three Pence Piece

Fig14.5: Silver Three Pence Piece 1918

- **Six pence**: 6d. Known as a 'tanner'. Silver coin, 19mm diameter.

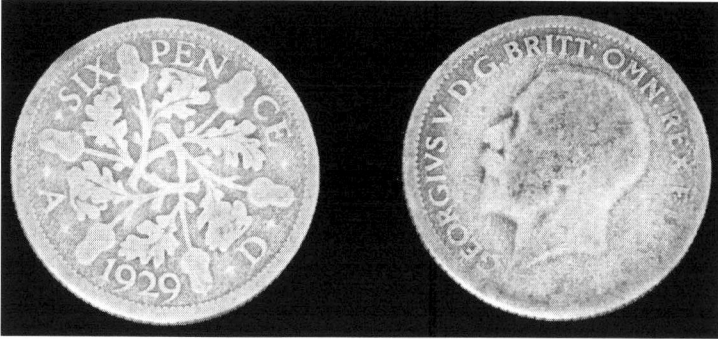

Fig 14.6: Sixpence piece 1929

- **Shilling:** 1/- or 1s. There were twelve pennies in the shilling and twenty shillings in the pound. A silver coin, 23mm diameter.

Fig 14.7: Shilling 1920

- **Florin**: 2/- or 2s. There were ten florins in the pound. A copper/nickel alloy coin, 28.5mm diameter.

Fig 14.8: Florin 1921

- **Half Crown:** 30d or 2s 6d (2/6). There were eight to the pound. A silver coin, 32mm diameter.

Fig 14.9: Half Crown 1921

- **Crown**: 60d or 5s (5/-). There were four to the pound. A silver coin, 38mm diameter.

- **Half Sovereign:** 10s (10/-). A 22ct gold coin and the **Sovereign**: 20s (20/-) or £1 were 22ct gold coins. Both have a much higher real value and have not been used as currency since Victorian times.

- **Groat**: (4d) was discontinued before the start of the twentieth century

In addition to the metal coins there were **Ten Shilling notes** (10/-), **One Pound notes** (£1) and **Five Pound notes** (£5) in circulation during the first four decades of the twentieth century.

14.1.2. Weights

Weights have also changed in recent times. The following is a rough guide.

- **1 ounce (oz) = approx 28 g**
- **1 pound (lb) = 16 oz = 0.45kg**
- **1 stone (st) = 14 lb = 6.35kg**
- **1 quarter = 2 st = 12.7kg**
- **1 hundredweight (cwt) = 4 quarters = 112 lb = 50.8kg**
- **1 ton =** 20 cwt = 2240 lb = 1016kg

14.1.3. Measures

- **1 fluid ounce (fl oz)** = approximately 28ml
- **1 gill** = 5 fl oz
- **1 pint (pt)** = 4 gills = 20 fl oz = approx. 568ml

- **2 pints** = 1 quart (approx. 0.9 litre)
- **1 quart** = 2 pt
- **1 gallon** = 4 quarts = 8 pt = 4.55 litres
- **1 peck** = 2 gallons = 9.1 litres

14.1.4. Measurements of Length and Distance

- **1 inch (in)** = 2.54cm
- **1 foot (ft)** = 12 in = approx. 30.5cm
- **1 yard (yd)** = 36 in = 3 ft = approx. 91.44cm
- **1 link** = 7.92in = 20.1 cm
- **1 rod** = 1 pole = 1 perch = 5.5 yds = 5.2m
- **1 chain** = 100 links = 22 yds = 4 poles = 2.1m
- **1 furlong** = 10 chains = 40 poles
- **1 mile** = 1760 yds = 80 chains = 8 furlongs = 1.6km
- **1 league** = 3 miles = 4.8km

14.2. Timeline of a few events that happened in Great Britain during the years 1901 – 1939

1901	**Jan:** Death of Queen Victoria. Accession of Edward VII
	Dec: First Transatlantic Radio Message.
1902	**Aug:** Coronation of Edward VII
	Sept: Harry Jackson becomes first person to be convicted on the evidence of fingerprints.
1903	Ebenezer Howard founded a company to develop the first "garden city" at Letchworth, Hertfordshire.
	Maximum speed limit set at 20 miles per hour. Before this regulations (1863) stated that motor engines could only proceed at 4 miles per hour and had to be preceded with man on foot waving a red flag.
	Oct: Women's Social and Political Union formed by Emmeline Pankhurst and her two daughters to fight for women's suffrage.
	Dec: Wright brothers' first flight lasted 59 seconds.
1904	**Jan:** *Daily Mirror* re-founded as ½ d illustrated newspaper.
	Jan: Number plates become compulsory on cars in Britain. They started with A1.
	Mar: Books of stamps go on sale for the first time, priced at 2s for 24 stamps.
	Britain's first permanent cinema built in London.
1905	**Jul:** Albert Einstein a 26 year old patent clerk, publishes 'A Special Theory of Relativity'.
	Oct: Aspirin goes on sale in British chemists.
1906	**Jan:** General Election. Liberals returned with overall majority of 85. 29 Labour MPs elected for first time.
	Mar: Rolls Royce Ltd, the car production company, formed and

	purchased a factory site in Derby.
	Apr: A severe earthquake in San Francisco kills 800 people.
	Oct: SOS becomes the International Distress Signal.
1907	**Jul:** Robert Baden-Powell initiates the Boy Scout movement with Camp at Brownsea Island.
	Qualification of Women's Act allowed women to become elected in borough and county council elections and as Mayor.
1908	**Jun:** England plays the first international football match against Austria, and wins 6-1.
	Jul: London hosts the Olympics.
1909	**Jan:** First state pensions paid to people over the age of 70 years.
	Jul: Louis Bleriot's first flight across the channel lasted 27 minutes.
1910	**Jan:** General Election. Minority Liberal government elected.
	May: Death of King Edward VII. Accession of George V.
1911	**Jan:** MPs become paid, allowing working class people to enter Parliament for the first time.
	Mar: The Shops Act entitles all shop employees to half-day holiday once each week.
	Apr: Population of Great Britain 36.1 million.
	Jun: Coronation of King George V held in London.
	Aug: Clashes between police and strikers mark Liverpool's "Bloody Sunday" on 13th August.
	Miners' strike lasts three months.
	Dec: Amundsen beats Captain Scott to the South Pole. Captain Scott and his team die on their return journey.
1912	**Apr:** The Sinking of the *Titanic*.
	May: London Dockers strike lasts three months.

	Jul: The Palace Theatre, London, hosts the first Royal Command Performance.
1913	**Jan:** some Britons become entitled to sickness and maternity benefits with the introduction of the National Insurance Scheme.
	May: Emily Davidson is killed when she steps in front of the king's horse at the Epsom Derby. Her funeral attended by 6000 marching Suffragettes.
1914	**Jun:** Assassination of Franz Ferdinand and his wife.
	Aug: Britain declares war on Germany.
	Aug: Press censorship introduced under the Defence of the Realm Act.
	Britain goes off the gold standard as a result of the war.
	Kitchener's "New Army" raised from volunteers.
1915	**Feb:** British Passports include photograph, signature and description of the holder for the first time.
	May: Formation of Coalition Government.
	May: sinking of the *Lusitania*, a liner carrying Americans
1916	**Jan:** Introduction of Conscription for all men between ages of 18 and 41.
	May: British Summertime introduced on a trial basis to save money on fuel.
1917	**Feb:** Women are permitted to drive taxis for the first time.
	Jun: The British royal family renounces all its German titles, changing its name from Saxe-Coburg-Gotha to Windsor.
	Sep: The RSPCA opens its first animal clinic.
1918	**Feb:** Representation of the People Act gives men over the age of 21 and women over 30 the right to vote.
	Apr: Royal Air Force created from the British Flying Corps. Air Board formed.

	Oct: The flu pandemic reaches Britain. It has already killed 25 million people across the world.
	Nov: Germany signs armistice with the Allies and fighting stops on the Western Front.
	Dec: Constance Markievicz became the first elected women MP (Sinn Fein), but she refused to take her seat in Parliament.
1919	**Jan:** Pensions raised to 10 shillings per week.
	Jun: Treaty of Versailles signed, settles the terms for peace.
	Dec: Viscountess Astor became the first woman MP to take up her seat in the House of Commons.
	Sex Disqualification Removal Act. Women were now allowed to work in all professions except the Church.
1920	Mar: The Automobile Association opens Britain's first petrol station in Aldermaston, Berkshire.
	Apr: Conscription was finally abolished.
	The first 'blue' British passports issued.
1921	Population 37.9 million
	Feb: Unemployment in Britain passes one million mark.
	May: The British Legion is founded to help struggling ex-servicemen.
	Jun: Postmen stop making Sunday deliveries.
	Apr – Jun: Miners' strike. State of emergency declared by government.
1922	**Oct:** Radio broadcasting begun by the British Broadcasting Company.
	Nov: Licences for radios introduced at 10s per year.
1923	Unemployment = 1.54 million
	Royal Tank Corps formed.

	Dec: General Election. Hung Parliament. Conservatives form government.
1924	Conservative government defeated. First Labour Government take office.
	Feb: BBC introduces 'pips' to pinpoint the exact point of the hour on radio.
	Feb: Baird transmits fist successful television pictures.
	Oct: Labour government defeated. General Election. Conservatives take office.
	Nov: Sunday Express publishes crossword puzzle, the first in a British newspaper.
1925	Unemployment = 1.22 million
	Mar: British Summertime made permanent.
	Apr: Britain returns to the gold standard.
	Oct: J Logie Baird successfully transmits the first greyscale moving television picture.
	Dec: Widows, Orphans and OAPs Act introduced contributory pensions at 65.
1926	Unemployment = 1.39 million
	Schools divided into "primary" and "secondary" with a transition at age 11.
	British Broadcasting Corporation set up as public operation designed to take over the radio broadcasts of the British Broadcasting Company.
	Jan: J Logie Baird's first public television demonstration.
	May: General Strike. 4,000 strikers were prosecuted and 1,000 imprisoned during the nine day general strike.
	May: Miners refuse wage cut and are locked out. Do not return to work until Nov.
	May: *British Gazette* produced (5th – 13th May) as an official

	government organ during the general strike. The TUC issue the *British Worker* (5th – 17th May) in response.
1927	Unemployment = 1.19 million
	Jan: Becomes possible to telephone New York from London at a cost of £15 for 3 minutes.
	May: Charles Lindbergh flew from New York to Paris – the first solo transatlantic crossing.
	The number of households that have a wireless radio licence reaches half a million.
1928	Unemployment = 1.21 million
	Mar: Representation of the People Act. The voting age of women reduced from 30 to 21. They now had the same restrictions on voting as men.
	Sep: The world speed record pushed above 300 miles per hour for the first time by Sir Malcolm Campbell in his car, Bluebird.
	Sep: Alexander Fleming discovers penicillin.
1929	**Mar:** Local Government Act abolished governors of the poor. County councils now had control in their place.
	May: General Election. Hung Parliament. Labour had most seats.
	Jun: Margaret Bondfield became the first female cabinet minister when she became Minister of Labour.
	Oct: Crash of the New York Stock Exchange (Wall Street Crash).
1930	Unemployment = 1.92 million
	Feb: Clyde Tombaugh discovers the ninth planet, Pluto.
	Jul: Mental Treatment Act. Voluntary treatment becomes possible for mental illness, to make it available to all classes, not just those who could afford the fees.
	Oct: R101 Airship crashes in France, killing 44 people.
	Oct: The Wall Street Crash had spread to Europe. By December

	2.5 million were unemployed.
1931	Unemployment = 2.63 million
	Jan: All speed limits on British roads are abolished – the reason given is that no one obeys them anyway!
	Apr: Ministry of Transport issues the first Highway Code.
	Jul: Trolley busses introduced in London.
	Sep: Britain leaves the gold standard and the pound is devalued.
	Oct: General Election. National Government voted in, with a Conservative majority.
	Oct – Nov: Widespread demonstrations against government economy measures. Clashes in Bristol, Salford, Manchester, Dundee and elsewhere.
1932	Unemployment = 2.7 million.
	Report by the Greater London Regional Planning Committee recommends a "green girdle" around London for recreational space that could be used by the public.
	Dec: George V gives the first Christmas Day broadcast by a British monarch.
1933	Unemployment = 2.52 million
	Jan: Hitler becomes Chancellor of Germany.
	Mar: Franklin D Roosevelt inaugurated as President of the United States of America.
1934	Unemployment = 2.16 million
	Jul: George V opens the 7 mile Mersey Tunnel.
1935	Unemployment = 2.03 million
	Mar: 30mph speed limit introduced in all urban area.
	Jun: Reconstruction of the National Government.
	May: Silver Jubilee of King George V and Queen Mary. Celebrations throughout the country. Included special Jubilee

	radio broadcast on May 6th by the King.
	Nov: General Election. National Government wins with large majority.
1936	**Jan:** Death of George V. Accession of Edward VIII.
	Nov: First talking television pictures broadcast from the Radio Exhibition in Olympia.
	Nov: Crystal Palace, London, burns to the ground.
	Dec: Abdication of Edward VIII, who takes the title the Duke of Windsor. Accession of George VI.
1937	Unemployment = 1.48 million.
	May: Frozen foods go on sale in Britain's shops.
	Jun: Duke of Windsor marries Wallace Simpson in France.
	May: Coronation of George VI.
	Jul: 999 emergency telephone number comes into operation.
	Salary for all Members of Parliament increased to £600 per annum.
1938	**Feb:** Nylon bristle toothbrush becomes the first commercial product made with nylon yarn.
	Jul: The first issue of *The Beano* published.
	Jul: The *Mallard* became the fastest steam locomotive in the world at almost 126 miles per hour.
1939	**Feb:** The first automatic car wash opens at a garage in Luton, Bedfordshire.
	Mar: Territorial Army doubled from 13 to 26 divisions.
	May: Conscription introduced.
	Sep: War declared on Germany.
	Sep: Television broadcasts suspended for the duration of the war.

14.3. Books published during the years 1901 - 1939

Books were expensive at the start of the century and remained that way until Penguin Paperbacks brought the novel to the mass market. These novels, some written in the previous century, were popular or first published in the year stated. We will all know many of them and still be reading them. If you haven't yet read them, they come highly recommended by many readers.

Date	Book	Author
1901	Kim	Rudyard Kipling
1902	The Hound of the Baskervilles	Arthur Conan Doyle
	Just So Stories	Rudyard Kipling
	The Way of All Flesh	Samuel Butler
1903	Man and Superman	George Bernard Shaw
1904	Peter Pan, or The Boy who wouldn't Grow Up	J M Barrie
1905	Kipps	H G Wells
1906	A Man of Property (first book in the Forsyte Saga)	John Galsworthy
1908	A Room with a View	E M Forster
	The Wind in the Willows	Kenneth Grahame
1910	Howards End	E M Forster
1912	Pygmalion	George Bernard Shaw
1913	Sons and Lovers	D H Lawrence
1914	Dubliners	James Joyce
	Tarzan of the Apes	Edgar Rice Burroughs
1915	The Thirty Nine Steps	John Buchan
	The Rainbow	D H Lawrence

	Of Human Bondage	W Somerset Maugham
1916	A Portrait of the Artist as a Young Man	James Joyce
1920	Women in Love	D H Lawrence
1921	Crome Yellow	Aldous Huxley
	The Mysterious Affair at Styles	Agatha Christie
1922	Ulysses	James Joyce
	The Waste Land	T S Elliot
	The Seven Pillars of Wisdom	T E Lawrence
1923	The Ego and The Id	Sigmund Freud
1924	A Passage to India	E M Forster
	The Vortex	Noel Coward
1925	Mein Kampf	Adolf Hitler
	Carry on, Jeeves	P G Wodehouse
	The Great Gatsby	F Scott Fitzgerald
	The Trial	Franz Kafka
1926	Winnie the Pooh	A A Milne
1927	Tarka the Otter	Henry Williamson
	To the Lighthouse	Virginia Woolf
1928	Lady Chatterley's Lover	D H Lawrence
	Orlando: A Biography	Virginia Woolf
	The House at Pooh Corner	A A Milne
1929	Goodbye to All That	Robert Graves
	A Farewell to Arms	Ernest Hemingway
1930	Diary of a Provincial Lady	E M Delafield

	Private Lives	Noel Coward
1931	All Passion Spent	Vita Sackville-West
	Cavalcade	Noel Coward
1932	Brave New World	Aldous Huxley
1933	Down and Out in Paris and London	George Orwell
	Natural Childbirth	Grantly Dick-Read
1934	Goodbye Mr Chips	James Hilton
	I, Claudius	Robert Graves
1937	The Hobbit	J R R Tolkein
1938	Brighton Rock	Graham Greene

14.4.   Songs from the Period.

We will all remember many of them. Some of the greats have been done many times by many different artists. After the advent of the radio music became a massive thing, with regular dances, records and the radio adding to their popularity. Of course, many of them came from the cinema too. Our parents, grandparents and ancestors would have been singing and clapping along to many of these tunes.

Date	Song	Sung By
1912	Everybody's Two Step	Billy Murray
1913	It's Nicer to be in Bed	Harry Lauder
1914	Aba Daba Honeymoon	Collins and Harlan
	The Little Ford Rambled Right Along	Billy Murray
1915	It's a Long Way to Tipperary	John McCormack
	I Didn't Raise my Boy to be a Soldier	Morton Harvey
1916	Santa Lucia	Enrico Caruso
	Keep the Home Fires Burning	James F Harrison
1917	A Batchelor Gay	Peter Dawson
	Over There	Nora Bayes
1918	After You've Gone	Marion Harris
	Over There	Enrico Caruso
1919	You ain't Heard Nothing Yet	Al Jolson
	I'm Forever Blowing Bubbles	Ben Selvin
1920	Crazy Blues	Mamie Smith
	Love Nest	John Steel
1921	Look for the Silver Lining	Marion Harris
	Wang Wang Blues	Paul Whiteman
	Margie	Eddie Cantor

1922	April Showers	Al Jolson
	Toot Toot Tootsie	Al Jolson
	Hot Lips	Paul Whiteman
1923	Yes! We Have No Bananas	Billy Murray
	Down Hearted Blues	Bessie Smith
1924	Show Me the Way to go Home	Ted Lewis
	The Prisoners Song	Vernon Dalhart
1925	Charleston	Paul Whiteman
	Yes, Sir! That's My Baby	Ace Brigode
1926	When the Red, Red Robin comes Bob, Bog, Bobbin' Along	Paul Whiteman
	Black Bottom	Johnny Hamp
	Do Do Do	Gertrude Lawrence
1927	Back Water Blues	Bessie Smith
	Ain't She Sweet	Gene Austin
	Broken Hearted	Paul Whiteman
1928	Ol' Man River	Bing Crosby
	I Wanna be Loved by You	Helen Kane
	Misbehave	Helen Kane
	Diga Diga Doo	Duke Ellington
1929	You were Meant for Me	Charles King
	Happy Days are Here Again	Johnny Marvin
1930	My Baby Just Cares For Me	Eddie Cantor in the film Whoopee!
	Dancing on the Ceiling	Jessie Matthews
	Puttin' on the Ritz	Harry Richman

	With a Song in My Heart	Lawrence Grey
1931	Dancing in the Dark	Bing Crosby
	Goodnight Sweetheart	Al Bawlly
	Sally	Gracie Fields
1932	Mad About the Boy	Antonia Wynn and Elsie Carlisle
	Night and Day	Cole Porter
	Teddy Bears' Picnic	Val Rosing
	Mad Dogs and Englishmen	Cole Porter
1933	You're Getting to be a Habit with Me	Bing Crosby
	Let's all sing like the Birdies Sing	Ben Bernie
	Stormy Weather	Ethel Waters
1934	Smoke Gets in Your Eyes	Turner Leyton
	Isle of Capri	Gracie Fields
	Stompin' at the Savoy	Chick Webb and his Orchestra
	Love in Bloom	Bing Crosby
	Lazy River	Hoagy Carmichael
1935	I'm in the Mood for Love	Frances Langford
	Blue Moon	Glen Grey
	A Fine Romance	Fred Astaire
	Red Sails in the Sunset	Guy Lombardo
1936	Alone	Tommy Dorsey
	Goody! Goody!	Ben Goodman
	The Glory of Love	Ben Goodman
1937	The Dipsy Doodle	Tommy Dorsey
	The Moon got in my Eyes	Bing Crosby

	That Old Feeling	Shep Fields
1938	Cry Baby Cry	Larry Clinton
	Thanks for the Memory	Shep Fields and Bob Hope

14.5.   Prime Ministers and Chancellors of the Exchequer.

Year	Prime Minster	Chancellor of the Exchequer
1900	Marquis of Salisbury	
1902	Earl of Balfour	Charles Thompson Richie (Lord)
1903		J A Chamberlain (Sir)
1905	Sir Henry Campbell-Bannerman	Herbert J Asquith (Earl)
1908	Herbert H Asquith (Earl of Oxford & Asquith)	David Lloyd George (Earl)
1910	Herbert H Asquith (Earl)	
1915		Reginald McKenna
1916	David Lloyd George (Earl)	Andrew Bonar Law
1919	J A Chamberlain (Sir)	Austin Chamberlain (Sir)
1921		Sir Robert Stevenson Horne (Viscount)
1922	Andrew Bonar Law	Stanley Baldwin (Earl)
1923	Stanley Baldwin (Earl)	Arthur Neville Chamberlain
1924(Jan)	James Ramsey MacDonald	Philip Snowdon (Viscount)
1924(Dec)	Stanley Baldwin (Earl)	Winston Leonard Spencer Churchill (Sir)
1929	James Ramsey MacDonald	Philip Snowdon (Viscount)
1935, 1936	Stanley Baldwin (Earl)	
1937	Neville Chamberlain	Sir John Allsbroke Simon (Viscount)

14.6.   Average Wages

Industry	1906	1924	1935
Skilled Workers			
Coalface Workers	112	180	149
Fitters	90	157	212
Engine Drivers	119	276	258
Compositors	91	209	218
Semi-Skilled and Unskilled			
Pottery Workers	77	171	173
Bus and Tram Drivers (London)	107	190	218
Agricultural Labourers	48	82	89
Clerical	**1911-13**	**1924**	**1935**
Civil Service Clerical Officer	116	284	260
Railway Clerk	76	221	224
Bank Clerk	142	280	224
Professional	**1913-14**	**1922-4**	**1935-7**
Barrister	478	1124	1090
General Practitioner	395	756	1094
Clergy	206	332	370
Manager	200	480 (1914-5)	440 (1938)

Average earnings for workers in pounds (£) per year (Stevenson, J: British Society 1914 – 1945 P121-122)

15.   Bibliography

This is a list of books that I have used when writing this book. They have provided a tremendous insight into the lives of our ancestors and the Social History of England and Wales:

Abbott, M *Family Affairs: A History of the Family in 20th Century England.* (2003) Routledge.

Bastable, J (Editor). *Yesterday's Britain: The Illustrated Story of how we Lived, Worked and Played.* (1998) Readers Digest.

Beeton, I. Ed. *Mrs Beeton's Book of Household Management.* (1861)

Cook, C & Stevenson, J. *The Longman Handbook of Modern British History 1714 - 1995.* (1996) Addison Westley Longman Ltd.

Gardiner, J. *The Thirties: An Intimate History*. (2010) Harper Press.

Hibbert, C. *The English: A Social History 1066 - 1945.* (1987) Harper Collins Publishers.

Horn, P. Ladies of the Manor. (1997) Sutton Publishing Ltd

Hopkins, E. A Social History of the English Working Classes 1815-1945. (1979) Hodder and Staughton Ltd

James, L. *The Middle Class, A History.* (2006) Abacus

Pearce, R. *1930s Britain.* (2010) Shire Living Histories

M Penber Reeves *Round About a Pound a Week* (1913) Virago Press

Poulton, R. *Kings and Commoners 1901 - 1936.* (1977) World's Work Ltd.

Pugh, M. *We danced all Night: A Social History of Britain Between the Wars.* (2009) Vintage Books.

Royle, E. *Modern Britain: A Social History 1750 - 1997.* (1997) Hodder Education.

Stevenson, J. *British Society 1914 - 45.* (1984) Penguin Books.

Taylor, A J P. *English History 1914 - 1945.* (1965) Oxford University Press.

Websites that have proved invaluable:

www.angloboerwar.com/boer-war

www.bbc.co.uk/news/10390469

http://en.wikipedia.org/wiki/Second_Boer_War#Concentration-camps_.281900.E2.80.931902.29

Http://www.1900s.org.uk/1900s-death-in-house.htm

Coins: www.predecimal.com/predecimaldenominations.htm.

Weights and Measures: http://gwydir.demon.co.uk/jo/units/length.htm

http://studymore.org.uk/mhhtim.htm#1839

www.beamish.org.uk/edwardian-christmas/

www.1900s.org.uk/1900s-Christmas-Preparations.htm

www.qlhs.org.uk/oracle/christmas-1900/christmas-1900.htm

www.dailymail.co.uk/femail/article-2607739/chocolate-chicken-pictures-1900s/easter-treats-youve-never-seen-shape-shoes-fish-poultry.htm

www.1900s.org.uk/1900s-may-day.htm

www.mkheritage.co.uk/ttm/telhistory1.htm

www.britishtelephones.com/histuk.htm

www.1900s.org.uk/1940s-images/postal-rates.jpg

http://en.wikipedia.org/wiki/Wright_brothers

http://en.wikipedia.org/wiki/Lunch

10926545R00107

Printed in Great Britain
by Amazon.co.uk, Ltd.,
Marston Gate.